THE TIME of MY LIFE

TRIUMPH AND TRAGEDY AT LONDON WEEKEND TELEVISION

PETER McNALLY

THE TIME
of MY LIFE

TRIUMPH AND TRAGEDY AT LONDON WEEKEND TELEVISION

MEMOIRS

Cirencester

Published by Memoirs

MEMOIRS
PUBLISHING

25 Market Place, Cirencester, Gloucestershire, GL7 2NX
info@memoirsbooks.co.uk www.memoirspublishing.com

Copyright ©Peter McNally, March 2013

First published in England, March 2013

Book jacket design Ray Lipscombe

ISBN 978-1-909544-55-0

Printed in England

CONTENTS

Introduction

The McNally Coat of Arms

To my family and many friends and former colleagues, in the hope that my memory has allowed me to relay accurately the significant events in my life. I apologise for any inaccuracy in these recollections.

Hannington Wick, March 2013

INTRODUCTION

Looking back over my life, I do not remember everything with pride or happiness. Some of the events which leave me embarrassed were moderate successes; others were dismal failures, most of which I would like to forget. I believe I was extremely lucky coming from a large and supportive family with devoted and loving parents whose concern was always for the wellbeing of their children rather than their own.

As my parents had both been privately educated, they were very keen that we should all be given the benefit of a public school education (an odd conflict in terms). This provided us all with a firm and confident base for the future, although it probably meant them going without holidays and other luxuries.

There is no doubt that the moral code and work ethic my brothers and I acquired in the years at Hodder and Stonyhurst have served us well in later life. The world doesn't owe us a living. Personal fulfilment and happiness can generally only come from our own efforts. This was probably helped by being a member of a large family, my mother being the eldest of eight children and her mother being one of ten, thus reducing the possibility of any significant financial inheritance. There was no doubt that if we were to enjoy the lifestyle of our grandparents we were going to have to overcome some significant challenges. As I was aware that there were many more intelligent and gifted individuals than myself, I realised I was going to have to work very hard and be very lucky, putting more time and effort into my business life without taking undue risks. It has paid off – I hope.

CHAPTER 1

BEGINNINGS
1933-39

I was born in March 1933 in Folkestone, Kent, the second of six children. My father, Patrick McNally, was a medical officer in the Royal Air Force. Both my parents came from large families. My father, who had been at school and university in Dublin, was one of five and came from an old Ulster family. My mother, the eldest of eight children, was born Mary Dean Outred. She was from a medical family with origins in Wiltshire. They had met when my mother was at finishing school in Belgium with my father's sister.

I have few memories of my early life, other than being constantly ill as a child. I was always being carted off to the local hospital in Gravesend, where my English grandfather practised as a GP. We lived in a series of rented houses, although some of these houses were provided by the RAF as my father moved from one posting to the next.

During my early years my father spent time in Iraq and was frequently away from England. When he was away on an overseas posting my mother took a house close to her family's home on the outskirts of Gravesend. During this time I remember that I was in and out of hospital on a pretty regular basis, mainly with asthma and bronchial problems – I was very much a weakling. These problems persisted into my early teenage years and I didn't really get over them until I had been for a couple of years at boarding school, not a very auspicious beginning.

At the time my mother was extremely fortunate to find an amazingly capable nanny to look after her ever expanding family. Her name was Stella, and she really was a star. I don't know what my mother would have done without her. She was exceptionally kind and wonderfully dedicated to the family.

Stella used to take us for long walks to the countryside around Gravesend. On one of these walks we saw a yellow biplane hurtling out of the sky and crashing into the woods. We wanted to go and see the wreckage, but Stella wisely would not let us get close to it. Could these have been training aircraft from Biggin Hill Air Base?

My English grandmother was a formidable lady, who had eight children and owned one of the first motor cars. This was in 1904, when the speed limit on roads was 20 mph. She always had servants and never learned to cook.

Grandmother was a Gilbert, a member of a large family with origins in the West Country. According to my mother she was descended from Sir Humphrey Gilbert, an Elizabethan venturer and half-brother to Sir Walter Raleigh.

The Gilberts traced the lineage back several centuries. Records show John Gilbert, Squire, living at Abbaston Manor, Shrewton, Wiltshire, in about 1600. The relationship to the Walter Raleigh Gilberts of Compton is a matter of conjecture, but it would seem likely that they were a branch of the same family. Great Aunt Lil wore a signet ring with a squirrel crest, which was common to both families. *Squirrel* was the name of a ship which was lost with Sir

Humphrey and his crew on the last of their voyages of discovery to North America.

In the 18th century Joseph Gilbert lost the family fortune, allegedly through gambling, and with it Abbaston Manor, which was then purchased by his aunt's family, the Miles. He was dead at the age of 28, but left two sons, Joseph Miles Gilbert, born in 1777, and the future General William, born in 1787. William was Colonel Commandant of the 21st Bombay Native Infantry, which in 1824 became a marine battalion. It was a regiment with a distinguished record of service, including the Afghan and Abyssinian campaigns. It also took part in repelling the Bombay Mutiny in 1858.

General William Gilbert lived in a house named Tweed in Hampshire. Apparently he remained a bachelor. In later years my Great Aunt Laura and her own child, Kit, used his uniforms for dressing up at parties!

His elder brother was grandfather to my grandmother, Mary Gilbert. Joseph, a highly-regarded marine artist, was commissioned to paint for Queen Victoria her review of the fleet during the early part of her reign. This painting was hanging at Osborne House, the then royal residence on the Isle of Wight. Joseph produced most of his work between 1825 and 1855; he exhibited at the Royal Academy during those years and lived in Westbourne Place, Chelsea, in the 1840s. This address no longer exists, having subsequently been renamed Clevedon Place. It leads into Sloane Square from Eton Square.

Joseph and his wife Lucy had one son, Thomas William, born in 1832. Thomas made his career in shipping and married Emma Biddlecombe, the daughter of an artist. They had nine children,

Humphrey, Charles, Lucy, Ellen, Kitty, Francis, George, Laura and my grandmother, Mary (May). They had homes in London and Hampshire; in Hampshire they lived in Pennington Place, near Lymington, which had extensive views over the marshes.

My grandmother and her sister Laura always regarded this as the family home. It was from there that my grandmother married her husband, Charles, and her sister Laura married her future husband, Robert Measures. In both cases the marriage ceremony was performed by their brother, Canon Francis Walter Gilbert, a distinguished priest who raised money to build his own church at Leigh on Sea with its own private crypt. He had planned to be buried in it, but was prevented from doing so by the local Bishop.

My grandfather set up practice in Gravesend and they too had a large family, eight children, of whom my mother was the eldest. She had three brothers and four sisters: Tom, Charles, Frank, Sally, Elizabeth, Dorothy and Anne. They lived in a large Victorian house in Gravesend with croquet lawns and tennis courts.

My mother was first sent away to school to the Convent of the Sacred Heart at Roehampton, together with her cousin Kit Measures (Great Aunt Laura's daughter, Laura Catherine Lucy). This school was attended by two of the most beautiful women of their generation, Vivian Leigh, who became Lady Olivier, and Maureen O'Sullivan (Jane of the Tarzan Films) before they escaped the claustrophobic confines of the convent to go to Hollywood.

Much of my mother's childhood was spent with her cousin Kit at Pipes Place. This was a William and Mary house with two home farms and several cottages. The house had been built in the 15th century by a Squire Parker, Sub Senechal of Gravesend, whose son had been under-steward to Oliver Cromwell. Behind the house the orchards rose up to a hill capped by four Douglas firs around a summer house overlooking the Thames estuary. The fire markers were used by ship pilots bringing large ships up to the port of London – a most obvious landmark.

Pipes Place, Shorne, 1953

The estate included an old vicarage and a forge, a walled garden and an extensive orchard. It had been bought by my Great Aunt Laura in 1919 after a devastating fire had destroyed her previous house, Creaksea Hall in Essex, with the loss of many of the family possessions. Her husband had died in 1912.

My grandmother's sister, Great Aunt Laura, had been married at the early age of 25 to 65-year-old Robert Measures. Great Aunt Laura was later remarried at the age of 43 to a Major John Cobb, an extremely distinguished yachtsman who had sailed on the Shamrock, the famous J class boat, with Sir Thomas Lipton.

My father's family lived in County Monaghan in Ulster. He had met my mother while she was staying there with his sister

Anne; the girls were at the same finishing school in Belgium. He was one of five children. He had an elder brother, Edward, a younger brother, John, and two sisters, Anne and Rochie. My grandparents were running a very successful linen business, with factories in Monaghan and Strabane.

According to my father, the family used to own a large part of Ulster. Rumour has it that one of his ancestors was responsible for betraying James I by changing sides at the Battle of the Boyne. Further research is clearly necessary, but the family does have a very warlike coat of arms! Apparently most of these lands had been forfeited in the early 1700s when one of his forebears had refused to sign the oath of allegiance.

Back in England I remember attending my first communion at the age of five, when I was sick at the communion breakfast. I also remember coming back to the house after church one Sunday with my mother to see a brand-new tricycle standing in the driveway of the house. As it was my fifth birthday I assumed it must be for me, though my mother and my elder brother, Charles, weren't quite so sure at first. It turned out to be a gift from my grandparents; a wonderful present, which I used to pedal up and down the drive shouting "my bicycle!" At least that's what my mother told me.

About this time we were vaguely aware of the rumblings of war. There were frequent visits from uncles and aunts to discuss with my mother the possible courses of action should war be declared.

My father had been running an RAF hospital in Iraq. In the same year, 1938, he was notified that his next posting would be to Shanghai. After extensive preparations for the whole family to move there, the posting was changed at the last minute and he was sent back to Iraq. In retrospect this was no bad thing, as he survived the war without injury.

CHAPTER 2

A BOY IN IRELAND
1939-1943

Soon after war was declared, it was decided at a family conference that the family should go to Ireland for the duration, a very fortunate decision for us. Accordingly, in 1939 we were all dispatched by train and boat across the Irish Sea.

Halfway across there was a major alert. We were awakened at the dead of night and bustled on deck with gas masks and life jackets on. In the distance we could see an aircraft dropping bombs in the sea. After an hour on deck the all-clear was sounded and we were allowed to go below. We all thought it was a great adventure and had no thought that we had just narrowly escaped from being torpedoed by a U-boat. It would not be the last lucky escape in my life.

When we first arrived in Ireland we stayed in one of the houses owned by my Irish grandparents. On one occasion, I can't understand for what reason, my elder brother decided to make a bonfire of all our toys, almost setting the house on fire. Perhaps this was his protest at being sent to one of the local schools, where, because of his English accent, he was given a very rough time.

Soon afterwards we moved to Poplar Vale, a lovely Georgian

farmhouse just outside Monaghan which was owned by an 'aunt', Miss Richardson. It had a drive which seemed to us at least a mile long and several hundred acres of grounds. We lived there with Stella the nanny and a series of governesses for some four years.

The farmhouse was a square-fronted brick building with an extensive cobbled yard and farm buildings behind. Poplar Vale was a glorious place to be, despite the absence of electric light and central heating. There were always peat fires to keep us warm during the winter in all the main rooms, even in our bedrooms. Lighting was by oil lamp throughout the house and we had a nightlight in our bedrooms at night. My mother was happy to have the family away from the bombings in England, and there was no shortage of food. My aunt employed a large staff – butler, cook, maids, etc – all being paid a pittance. The maids were paid five shillings (25p) a week all found.

There was a courtyard at the back of the house, in the centre of which was a wheel from which extended a long wooden tiller – similar to that of a lock gate – which was used to operate a device which churned the milk to make butter in the kitchen. A farm horse was attached to the tiller and walked round the courtyard. The only time I have seen a similar device was in Rajasthan in India, where it was used to pump water from wells to irrigate the fields. Could it be that my aunt's grandfather, who was in the Indian army, had brought back the idea to Ireland?

My mother, a devout Catholic, did have a problem with schooling. Apparently the only good local school was Church of Ireland and the local Roman Catholic bishop was not keen on the idea of us being sent there. She therefore engaged a series of governesses so that I and my three brothers, Charles, John and Patrick, and my sister Rosemary could be taught at home.

Unfortunately none of these governesses stayed with us very long. I suspect we developed a technique for accelerating the departure of each one in turn! I remember there was one we really liked, but even she only lasted a few weeks. We really must have been terrible children. As a result we were all semi-literate on being sent to boarding school in England in 1943.

A number of incidents occurred during the four years in Ireland, one or two of which I remember. My brothers Charles and John, had taken a dislike to the lady who lived in one of the cottages near the main house. We had discovered in one of the attics a number of old swords and lots of old letters and envelopes, most of which had Victorian red or black stamps, probably priceless today. We decided to launch an attack on the woman. My brothers and I each took a sword and marched in line along the driveway towards the door of the cottage. When we got to within 20 yards of the door she opened it and chased us down the drive with a broomstick. We abandoned our swords in the bushes and ran back to the main house.

Later that day my aunt, clearly having heard this sorry tale, asked me to show her where the swords had been thrown away. Together she and I gathered them up and took them back to the house. It was not a very good day for my long-suffering mother!

Another day we were all out walking in the country lane near the house with my mother and nanny when we looked through the hedge to see a white goat giving birth to two babies. We did not have any pets, so we all begged and implored my mother to buy the two baby goats for us. The local farmer was delighted and sold them to her at sixpence each, but we could not collect them for two weeks. My mother was incensed that when she went to collect them she was charged 18 pence each. The farmer was including the cost of the milk consumed in the two weeks prior to collection.

The goats became wonderful pets. For several weeks, until they could eat grass, they had to be fed each day from a bottle. There was never any shortage of volunteers. Consequently they became great friends and totally attached to the family.

Eventually the male became rather aggressive and started butting my younger brothers and sisters, so he had to be sold. We swapped him for two doves, which immediately flew away. But the nanny goat was a delightful pet. She was never happier than when going for walks with us. On one occasion when she saw us going for a walk without her she was so desperate to follow us that she got her collar caught through the top spike of the gate to the stall. Luckily we managed to free her with some help from the farm manager, and she was not hurt.

When I was about eight I was in bed with a cold. Waking up in the middle of the night I could see by the light of the candle a tall lady dressed in a magnificent white dress standing at the foot of my bed. She stood there for several minutes and then disappeared. I thought it must be my mother or aunt, or Stella. In the morning I asked which one it was and where the wonderful white dress had come from, as I had never seen it before. They all denied that any of them had been near my room that night and none of them had such a white dress. To this day the image is as clear as it was then. Was I dreaming, or had I really seen a ghost?

About that time Charles and John persuaded me to buy some cigarettes – a little packet of five Woodbines. They told me that to get the full pleasure I had to smoke the whole lot. Although they were very thin cigarettes, after about three I felt seriously ill and was very sick. My mother wasn't aware of the purchase of the cigarettes and was so concerned that she took me to the doctor.

After a lengthy examination, not finding any reason for my vomiting, he asked "Could your son have been smoking?" My mother replied "What, at five years old?" That 5p investment was a really good one, as it put me off smoking for the rest of my live and saved me a lot of money.

Poplar Vale is now an agricultural college and my old room is a passageway to a modern dormitory.

Another incident occurred while we were all out for a walk one day, together with the nanny, my mother and the goat. We came across a group of riders out hunting. They turned out to be my grandparents, all mounted on lovely horses. During the meeting my grandfather gave me a half sovereign as a belated birthday present. When my mother discovered this she insisted I return it to him, as it was an enormous sum in those days. I was really disappointed and at first refused to do so.

After that we all wanted to learn to ride. The horses at my grandparents' stables were all too big, so we had to content ourselves with riding the small pony that was normally used to drive the trap which took us to church in Monaghan every Sunday and other shopping trips into town. Sometimes my grandfather sent his car and chauffeur to pick us up and take us to tea. He never shaved himself and could not drive.

My Irish grandparents owned a number of properties in Ireland, including the Belle Broid Linen factory in Monaghan. At the beginning of the century this business had been started by my grandparents to give employment to a number of Belgian refugees who had come to Ulster in the early 1900s. My grandmother, who had been at finishing school in Belgium, was a fluent French speaker, and she and my grandfather had founded a very successful business manufacturing, embroidering and selling linen to the UK. They had started two factories, one in Strabane and one in Monaghan. This allowed manufacturing to take place both in Northern Ireland and in the Irish Republic. In the thirties it had been enormously successful, but the war changed everything when the demand for this luxury product disappeared. The operations were reduced significantly and the factory in Strabane closed.

Monaghan was one of the three Ulster counties which, because of the large Catholic population, was not included with the other six counties of Ulster which became Northern Ireland in 1922. Had they been included, the Catholic population in Northern Ireland would have been close to 50% of the total rather than 33%.

My grandmother's family, the Gallaghers, had extensive property interests in Ireland and England, including Urney Chocolates and Suttons of Reading. One of her cousins owned the 1964 Derby winner Santa Claus, so Christmas came early that year!

At Poplar Vale the farm manager, a friendly man, was assisted during the harvest and at Christmas by a number of workers from one of the local lunatic asylums – there were three of them. At Christmas a large number of chickens and geese in the farmyard had to be killed and plucked. There was a particularly aggressive goose in the farmyard who would chase us children, honking loudy, if we got too near.

We children sometimes tried to help with the plucking. I remember one of the lunatic pluckers handing me a chicken with its head tucked under its wing. As I held it, it escaped – obviously I hadn't held it tightly enough. On another occasion, when the neck of the chicken had been wrung and was hanging off, the chicken jumped out of the plucker's hand and rushed round the farmyard headless.

Living in Ireland was a wonderful experience, with acres of fields to play in with the farm animals and total liberty from any form of supervision.

One day John and I decided we would find out whether cats really had nine lives. We prepared a fire, dowsed liberally with oil destined for the lamps in the house and some shotgun cartridges from the farm office. We put the cat on the top of the pile and were just about to set light to the bonfire when, luckily for the cat, the farm manager discovered us. That experiment was not very successful. The next attempt to test the nine-lives theory involved throwing the cat out of a third-floor window, when it succeeded in running down the wall and escaping, totally uninjured. After that we decided it really must have nine lives.

In addition to the tame cats around the house there were a large number of wild ones roaming the grounds and feeding on the rats and mice in the farm buildings. This necessitated the farmer frequently having to drown new offspring, which he did by putting them in a sack with some stones, dropping the sack into a barrel of water and leaving it there for five to ten minutes. We children were horrified, and were always trying to save the little kittens. Even so, the number of cats around the house and in the grounds was always increasing.

Rats were always getting into the house. On one occasion a rat got into the drawing room and was cornered. The butler was trying to hit it with a poker, but the rat shot out of the corner into the air over my shoulder and escaped, only missing my face by a couple of inches. There is nothing more dangerous than a cornered rat. A lucky escape for all.

We children had been told by the farm manager that you could catch a rabbit by putting salt on its tail. For a number of days we went walking in the woods with a packet of salt, eventually managing to hit the tail of a passing rabbit – no mean feat for a seven-year-old. Not surprisingly, it didn't stop to be caught. An early lesson on not to believe everything one is told!

In 1943 my mother had her last child. I then had three brothers and two very special younger sisters, Rosemary and Maryanne.

CHAPTER 3

SCHOOLDAYS AND SCRAPES
1943-1949

In 1943, once America had joined the war, the family returned to England, which was then judged to be a safer place. My brother Charles and I were immediately sent to Hodder Place, the preparatory school for Stonyhurst in Lancashire. It proved to be a baptism of fire. Having run wild in Ireland for four years totally unsupervised and wholly unused to any form of formal schooling, we were always in hot water. Although we could just about read and write, we were way behind the other boys, which put us at a considerable disadvantage.

Hodder Place was and is an extremely charming stone-built country house, which in those days accommodated about 60 boys. It had a Jesuit headmaster aged about 69, who had probably been brought out of retirement. He was known affectionately as Poppa Weld and was a descendant of Sir Thomas Weld, who in 1798 had donated the estate at Stonyhurst to the Jesuits. The school had been located in a series of different places and in 1790 it had been thrown out of St Omer in France, where I understand the Jesuits did not head the popularity league.

By today's standards the régime was extremely strict, with

15

physical punishment liberally dispensed to wrongdoers. The principal instrument of punishment was the 'ferula'. This consisted of a piece of whalebone encased in leather and administered on one's left hand in units of three, six or nine, or in exceptional circumstances, for the most serious offence, twice nine.

At that time my father was still stationed in Egypt and my mother had taken a house in Shoeburyness to be near one of her four sisters. This was my Aunt Dot Tolhurst, an accomplished horsewoman and county tennis player.

We were dispatched by train from London, where we were met and taken by coach to Hodder for my first term. Hodder Place was in a delightful position next to the River Hodder, overlooking a beautiful wooded valley and some three or four miles away from the nearest town, Clitheroe. As we had come from the depths of the equally attractive Irish countryside, its beauty was probably lost on my brothers and me at the time, but that did not prevent the river from casting a spell which would entrance me for the rest of my life.

The school rugby field, called Paradise, was situated between the school and the river, and the cricket pitch was on the field on high ground just above the school. The river flowed in a deep valley just behind the school, where there were some old stone bathing huts.

My father in his younger days had played rugby and boxed for his university, University College Dublin, and during his leave from Iraq and Egypt he was keen to pass on some of his skills to us. As a result we had practised kicking, tackling and running with the ball in the garden of the house my parents had rented near Preston. Consequently when I arrived at Hodder I was able to claim, without much justification, that I could play rugby, having practised passing and tackling on the lawn at home. This aroused a lot of hilarity, both from my fellow pupils and rugby master, and made me determined to succeed and to prove them all wrong. I'm pleased to say I was able to do so.

At the end of the first term, by which time I had beaten my elder brother's record for receiving the maximum number of ferulas – a record to be further exceeded by my younger brothers, John and Paddy – the school was assembled on the Sunday after mass to be addressed by the headmaster. In his address before we had left for the holidays, the headmaster, apart from his usual admonition to study during the holidays and return safe and sound, had explicitly instructed us on no account to bring back any matches to school.

We departed back to our families to endure the rigours of rationing – a first for our family, as being in Ireland we had not lacked for anything in the way of food. As a consequence we were probably a lot healthier and stronger than most of our classmates, although having suffered from bronchitis and asthma as an infant I was probably not the strongest. The concept of ration books and clothing coupons was a totally new one. We had to take them back to school each term.

Arriving back to Hodder for the second term, I decided to supplement my meagre pocket money – I think it was five shillings a term – by a little entrepreneurial activity. Having been forbidden to bring back matches I thought they would be in extremely short supply, so I spent most of my pocket money on a dozen boxes, which I hoped to sell at a considerable profit.

On the school train, where several compartments had been reserved for the boys coming back to school, I was demonstrating a number of tricks to be performed with lighted matches to potential "buyers" from my class. I was in the midst of a demonstration which involved flicking a lighted match with a finger across the carriage compartment when the horrified master in charge of the school carriages caught me in mid-flow.

Needless to say the business venture was a flop and I had hardly any pocket money that term. Worst of all was the assembly on the first Sunday, when we were addressed by the headmaster. After welcoming us all back he had to tell us of the most frightening and horrendous incident that had occurred on the school train coming back from the holidays, involving one of us boys. I began to realise what was coming next!

"One boy has had the impudence and temerity to totally disregard which I specifically forbade you all to do at the end of last term. He brought back matches. Not one box, but a dozen! Stand up McNally minor!" A very red-faced McNally minor duly stood up. The Head continued at length, me getting redder and redder, and finished by ordering me to write 1000 lines and have nine ferulas as punishment. Quite a relief, as I had expected the ultimate – twice nine. But I hated doing the lines. I think I would have preferred to have the twice nine and escape the lines. However, it did establish my reputation at the junior school!

My reputation was further enhanced when I was chosen to play fullback for the Hodder rugby team against the junior Stonyhurst rugby 15. Although we lost by six points to three, having saved a large number of tries through low tackling (as taught by my father) I was carted off the field on the shoulders of my team-mates – most embarrassing, but very satisfactory.

I was less successful at cricket. It was only after being bowled out frequently without scoring that I became aware that my master eye was my left rather than my right. After that, batting improved enormously, although cricket was never really my favourite game. Rugby was something I thoroughly enjoyed, probably because I was good at it.

Scholastically things did not work quite as well. Latin and French were always a problem, but I was catching up with the rest of the class in all the other subjects. Luckily for my older brother Charles and me, success at school in those years was based on sporting rather than scholastic achievement. Charles was an exceptional athlete and excelled in all things physical - particularly when we fought.

The first two terms were not particularly happy ones. I was away from the family for the first time and received regular punishment for the most minor of offences, such as reading by torchlight after dormitory lights were off. Both the dormitories at Hodder and Stonyhurst were located in large top-floor rooms. The rooms were equipped with wooden partitions approximately six and a half feet by four and a half, separating each bed. There was just enough room for a small bedroom table and cabinet, with clothes stored in enormous chests of drawers in the centre of the room. There was a curtain at the end of the bed, which provided some privacy.

I had been having a very rough time with one of the staff, a senior master, and had made a small wax effigy of him. One evening after lights out I was in the process of sticking pins into the wax figure by torchlight under the blankets when I was discovered. More trouble. There was talk of expulsion and black magic. I escaped with another nine ferulas.

During our time at Hodder our parents frequently gave up their rations to send sweets and chocolates. However these had to be handed in and were then distributed to all boys, a practice which meant we didn't get the chocolates our parents had carefully saved for us, so we asked our mother not to send us any more but to keep them for the holidays.

Hodder Place is no longer a school. It has now been divided into flats, while St Mary's Hall has now become the preparatory school for Stonyhurst, but I'm told that the boys still come and swim in the river at Tiddy Wheel, next to the Paradise rugby field.

There was strict petrol rationing at that time, so parental visits during term were infrequent. I still remember my father arriving on the back of a motorcycle to visit us at school and take us out to tea in one of the village cottages which specialised in high teas.

It was probably during the summer holidays before I went to Stonyhurst that I caught pneumonia while we were staying in Shoeburyness. I became extremely ill and nearly died. I even remember receiving the last sacraments from the local priest, though I was not told this at the time. I was so delirious that mother gave me hot whisky and honey and lemon to help me to sleep. It must have been just after the advent of penicillin, discovered by Sir Alexander Fleming. Luckily I recovered and went back to the school with the daily requirement of cod liver oil and malt. The illness left me extremely weak, and I was determined to improve my physique by regular exercise.

The transition from Hodder to Stonyhurst was a smooth one, as most of the boys went automatically from the junior school to the senior school, complete with their school reports and their reputations. It was for me a happy transition, as by this time I had learned to avoid punishment, or rather to avoid being caught.

One of my school friends had written off for an exercise course called the Charles Atlas Course, whose sales pitch included the slogan "Why be a seven stone weakling when you could be a real man?". He had paid good money for the course and generously agreed to let me see the recommended exercises, which were entitled "dynamic tension". I practised these exercises each morning and evening for several years, with remarkable results. Good old Charles Atlas.

Life at Stonyhurst became more enjoyable than at Hodder. To start with I had learned to play by the rules – it probably helped that as my strength improved I was able to play an increasingly useful part on the rugby field and in the school boxing team. In this I was encouraged by the sports master, Flt. Sergeant Keating, who was particularly helpful, probably because I was the son of an RAF doctor. The development of my arm and chest muscles had helped to overcome the asthmatic problems and was particularly useful in the boxing ring and in cross-country running.

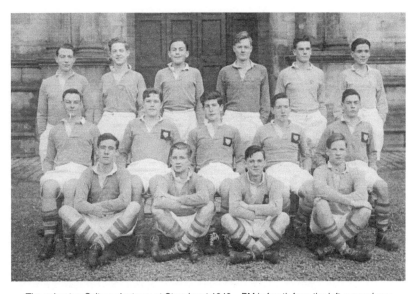

The unbeaten Colts rugby team at Stonyhurst 1948 – PM is fourth from the left, second row

School photo, 1948 - PM second row, seated right. Brother Charles
is in the third row in front of the statue

On a cross-country steeplechase, PM jumping the hedge

My father had boxed and played rugby for his school, Blackrock, and his university, University College Dublin, and I wanted to do the same. As a result of Keating's training I never lost a boxing match against a number of schools, although one match ended in a draw. On one occasion in a match against Denstone, a local school, we lost the first six of the thirteen matches and won the last seven to win the match overall. After the last bout the father of one of the Denstone boys was so impressed that he asked whether his son could come to Stonyhurst.

Pocket money in those days was never enough. One way this could be supplemented was by playing cards, something we had learned to do as a big family using matches rather than money. The favoured game was vingt-et-un, a form of blackjack, where I had discovered a set of golden rules which led to either the bank or the punter being in the position to make money. The key to winning, if one were holding the bank, was to insist on a very small difference between the highest and the lowest opening bet. The reverse was the case if you were in the position of punter. As a result I became quite proficient at the game, and this became a great help in supplementing my meagre pocket money.

When I was fifteen I found myself in the same class as my elder brother Charles, Syntax II. This was the second stream and included a number of older, less academically gifted, boys and the younger ones – myself included – who had not quite made it into the first stream. It must have been very distressing for my brother Charles to be in the same class, as I was eighteen months his junior, although it didn't seem to faze him very much at the time. It was in Syntax II that we took our matriculation exams. My weak subjects were Latin and French. Luckily I made up for it in mathematics, algebra, geography, history, English (literature and language) and science (chemistry and physics) – anyway, enough to pass my matriculation.

It was probably about this time that we acquired the habit of putting our school books in a pile on the top of our desks to ensure that the master at the front of the class couldn't see what we were doing behind them. One of the tricks we boys used to play on each other was to push another boy's books over just before the arrival of the master, so that the unfortunate boy would be on the floor picking up his books as the master arrived and wasn't able to retaliate. On one occasion when that happened to me, just as I had retrieved the last book from the floor the culprit, John Pettit, pushed the whole pile over again on my head. Seeing red, I punched him, hitting him with such force just above his right eye that I not only cut his forehead but damaged my right fist, breaking the knuckle in my right hand.

A minute later the master arrived, not noticing at first that anything was wrong, as by this time all the books had been retrieved. John just sat there with blood dripping from his forehead and forming a pool on his desk top. The master soon had him off to the infirmary to have the cut tended to. After that I don't think anybody played that trick on me again, but I am still short of a knuckle on my right hand!

One of the games played in the playground was "hot rice", which is a form of French cricket played with a pot stick (a narrow baseball-type bat) and a tennis ball, played by three boys. The idea was to hit the "batsman" below the knees with the ball, the batsman defending himself with his pot stick. If you could give the ball a really good whack you stood a chance of staying in a while.

Otherwise the other players got very close and by throwing the ball quickly to each other they could have you out in no time.

The great joy for me of the summer term was the visits to the river Hodder to fish for trout and salmon. Occasionally the whole class would spend an afternoon swimming and picnicking beside the river.

In those days sport was regarded as an important part of the essential schooling of boys, as was membership of the Combined Cadet Force (CCF). Participation in all the main sports was therefore compulsory, whether you liked it or not and however competent or otherwise you were, so rugby, cricket and cross-country running all had to be endured. Success at games was also the means by which the success of the school was measured by other schools, while individual status was judged more by ability on the rugby field or on the cricket pitch than by academic achievement. In those days entry to Oxbridge was relatively easy compared to today. A good rugby or cricket player could obtain entry with reasonable, but not exceptional, exam results.

The coaches for the under-16 rugby team (the Colts) were a Father Tranmar and a Mr St Laurence, one coach for the forwards (the scrum) and the other for the backs. I was lucky enough to play wing forward, not having quite the acceleration to play in the backs or on the wing, and found myself in the Colts unbeaten rugby team in the year when the Stonyhurst first team won the Middlesex seven-a-side tournament at Richmond; it was 1948. As a result of this and my membership of the school boxing team, with my unbeaten record, I was allowed to go fishing during the summer term instead of playing cricket, in which I'd never been particularly proficient. This was a great privilege. When my classmates had to take part in cricket practice I would put on my running shoes, sprint down to the Hodder some two miles away (it took about twenty minutes), fish for an hour or so and run back to the college. As a result of this I was very fit, which helped a lot in preparing me for cross country running.

Occasionally the trips to the river were more relaxed, and we made fires to cook the few trout I managed to catch. On a number of occasions I would bring the trout back to the college kitchen and they would do a special fish supper for me and my friends.

The other activity we carried out at the river was spearing eels. During the summer it was possible to find them lurking under the large stones in the shallow water of the river, away from the main current. If we moved the stone very gently sideways we could sometimes see the head of an eel poking out. The trick was to spear the eel just behind the head with a specially sharpened and straightened fork. You had to use a lot of force to ensure that the eel was impaled on the fork and held on the bottom of the river. The wielder of the fork had to be very quick and accurate and hold on very tightly, otherwise the eel would escape. You had to skin the eel before cooking it on the riverbank. This was done by cutting off the head, then holding the end of the skin in one's teeth and pulling the body away until the skin peeled away from the body. Not surprisingly it did not do my teeth any good, and may well have contributed to the unevenness of them. I seem to remember that we had more eels than trout.

In those days the River Hodder was quite clear until it joined the River Calder at Hodder Foot, which often flowed white or green with industrial effluent. Since then I believe the Calder has been cleaned up and there has been a revival of the runs of salmon and sea trout. As a consequence there has been a reduction in the number of brown trout. Some of my happiest times at Stonyhurst were spent in the river at Tiddy Wheel.

In my final year at school, discussion started with my parents about career prospects. My initial thoughts were to follow the family tradition of medicine. There were a lot of doctors in the family, and my English grandfather was not only a doctor but a qualified dentist. My father and one of his brothers were doctors, as were two of my mother's. Additionally one of my mother's four sisters had married a doctor.

There was also the offer of a place at Cambridge, but this could not be taken until September 1951 when I was 18½ years old. My father was very unenthusiastic about the prospects for medicine under the National Health Service. I think he was also apprehensive at the prospect of supporting me for another seven years to the age of 25. With six children to educate, he was keen that I should be earning as early as possible. Additionally, being one of six it would be most unlikely that I would inherit any money from the family. Could I not find a profession where I had a greater chance of making money, where the training was not so long and I would not be a liability for him for seven years? If he were to put me through medicine he would have to do the same for the other five children, if they so wished – he still had four of us at private schools and would be paying school fees for the next ten years!

The logic was convincing. Soon afterwards I had a call from my uncle Frank, a qualified solicitor, who was managing director of a family structural engineering company in London, Measures Brothers (1911) Ltd. He invited me to lunch at his club in Holborn. Over a most enjoyable lunch he asked me what I wanted to do as a career after leaving school. Obviously he had been talking to my parents.

PM's father Patrick with the Princess Royal at Ely Hospital

I told him I would like to become a doctor, but was concerned at the length of time it would take to qualify. He commented that to do so would require some competence in Latin, which was not my strongest subject, and furthermore I would not be earning a salary until I was 25.

"What about law?" I asked. "You are a solicitor, and that takes only five years." Again he commented that Latin would be an important requirement.

"What about architecture?"

"Full of long-haired theorists" he said. "Very difficult to make money as an architect." (As I found out in later years.)

"What about engineering?" I asked.

"A lot of grease monkeys, not a profession for a gentleman" he responded.

"A barrister?"

"Are you quick on your feet? And what about your weakness in Latin?"

He then asked if I had ever considered becoming a chartered accountant. At the age of 16 I had barely heard of accountancy, let alone considered it as a profession. The mental image of a chartered accountant to me at that time was a little bald man sitting on a high stool writing in a large ledger with a quill pen. Not a very appealing prospect.

He went on to explain that accountancy was the profession of the future, as in those days very few businessmen had any sort of formal training. It was in his view the best training ground for future captains of industry, and once qualified the world would be my oyster. It only took five years' training and I could start on my 17th birthday in March next year. It was quite an attractive prospect for the family finances.

After that he looked at his watch and told me to drink up my coffee, as we had an appointment in the city in fifteen minutes' time. He had organised an interview with a charming gentleman called Lieutenant Colonel Cyril Oscar Skey, partner in a medium-sized firm of chartered accountants in Throgmorton Avenue, Cassleton Elliott & Co. He was the partner in charge of recruitment and told me that I could have as much time off during my five years' articles for sport, and they only took pupils from the best public schools. He did a great selling job, including the promise of £100 per annum and no need to pay a premium for the articles. At that time quite a number of firms of accountants insisted on a premium payment for articles, which was then repaid over the period of study.

Leaving school at the end of the Christmas term in 1949 meant that I was departing some 18 months earlier than most of my contemporaries. As a result I missed out on being a monitor and taking the higher certificate examinations. However, I was already in the first fifteen rugby team and the school boxing team, and the prospect of being self-supporting by the age of 22 was very appealing.

CHAPTER 4

A NEW WORLD

1950 -1955

∾

I left school in December 1949 with a mixture of regret and excitement, and joined Cassleton Elliott early in 1950.

At that time my mother and father were based in Ely, Cambridgeshire, where my father had just been appointed commanding officer of the RAF hospital. It was a particularly attractive posting, as at that time the CO was entitled to an eight-bedroom house with a number of house staff, including a gardener and chauffeur.

On the staff of the hospital was an Irish dental surgeon whose brother lived during the week at a boarding house in Islington in Belitha Villas. By sheer good fortune the landlady, the unfortunately-named Mrs Looney, had a vacancy and I was welcomed into her establishment on a Monday-to-Friday basis for the princely sum of two guineas per week (£2 2s), breakfast and supper included.

The accommodation proved to be quite small. My room measured approximately 9 ft x 12 ft with a desk, a chair and jug and basin and shared use of a bathroom one floor down on the half landing. Islington was, however, ideally placed to get to the city by tube or bus at the cost of 2½ pence (roughly 1p in today's currency) and Cassleton Elliott provided us with luncheon vouchers to the value of two shillings and sixpence per day (12½ pence). For this one could buy a steak and kidney pie and coffee at Lyon's Corner House.

At Cassleton Elliott there were approximately ten partners and ten articled clerks, and of these I remember three particularly – Tom Manners, Alistair McKillop and Michael Savage, all of whom were a couple of years older than me but very friendly. Keen on shooting and fishing and other country sports, Tom was the grandson of a duke, so he was a little grander than the rest of us. My fellow pupils were an extremely charming and civilised bunch, most of them having enough money not to go too hungry. As a result not all of them finished the course.

As we were all being paid a pittance, we did not feel it necessary to over-exert ourselves during the working day. We all had to do serious study when we got home from work in the evening, and in the early years the work was extremely repetitive and not at all stimulating. One of the advantages of coming straight from school without a break was that it was relatively easy to adopt a work and study routine. Had I not had my National Service deferred before entering the city, I think it would have been very difficult to adjust afterwards to working during the day and studying in the evening.

As most of my friends were still at school, the first three years of articles were extremely boring and uneventful. Social life was also very limited, although I did join the London Irish Rugby Club. Because of my relative youth and lack of bulk at 10½ stone, I could not join the first 15, so I had to be content with occasional appearances with the second London Irish team, the "Wild Geese".

In those days London Irish had about seven or eight teams, and the objective appeared to be to build up enough thirst to be able to drink at least ten pints of beer after the game. I soon realised that I was not going to make it to county or international level, and after a couple of years I gave up playing regularly. I did not like beer that much!

I did however enjoy the singsongs at the end of the evening. Such songs as *The Ball at Kerrymuir* were a regular feature, but there was one that stopped the visiting teams in their tracks. It had been adapted by Dr Cormick Swan from the nursery song *Christopher Robin*. It went as follows:

> *Little boy kneels at the foot of the bed*
> *Droops on his little hand, little gold head*
> *Hush, hush, whisper who dares*
> *Christopher Robin is saying his prayers.*
> *God bless mummy, I know that is right*
> *And God help daddy, it's Saturday night*
> *He is out playing rugby, he will be in a state*
> *And mummy will bash him if he is late*
> *I heard mummy say it's a terrible game*
> *He will only come home drunk and lame*
> *It's only an excuse to get out of the house*
> *And spend all his money on drink – the louse!*
> *The key is turning, the door opens wide*
> *Now Christopher's daddy has fallen inside*
> *His tie is undone and he has lost his cap*
> *Daddy is vomiting all over the mat*
> *When I grow up I will be like dad*

I will drink and sing and will be glad
But nobody will say a word to me
For I won't marry at all, you see.
Little boy kneels at the foot of the bed
Droops on his little bed, little gold head
Hush, hush, whisper who dares,
Christopher's daddy has fallen downstairs!

I tried to get home to Ely at the weekends to see my family, although the rail fare took a lot out of my meagre income. In those days I was always short of money. With total income of around £5 per week (which included £3 from my parents) and fixed outgoings of at least £3.50 a week there was not much surplus, and I found it very hard to make ends meet. Occasionally I was lucky enough to get a lift up to Ely at the weekends from Anthony Buck, a trainee barrister, later to become a member of the Conservative Cabinet. I was also lucky enough to be invited down for some weekends with my Great Aunt Laura in Kent. I enjoyed these weekends on her estate and was able to roam the land with a borrowed gun in the hope of bagging the odd partridge or rabbit. There was a little summerhouse on the top of a hill behind the main house where a large number of pigeons used to roost in the evening, which provided some very exciting sport.

When I was 19 I passed the intermediate chartered accountancy exam. Soon afterwards I moved from Islington into a large basement flat in Westbourne Grove with two friends, Shaun Dowling and John Vigurs, both of whom I had met playing rugby. It was a large flat with a big garden. Soon after moving in we met a group of party-loving Old Stoaks (Stow old boys). Key members of this group included Michael Shurey, who had just left the Coldstream Guards, and Tim and Henry Morris, a most amusing and entertaining pair. Directly they found we had such a big flat they suggested it was a perfect place for a party, and Tim set about organising one the next evening. That started a series of twice-weekly parties, and my circle of friends expanded rapidly.

It was probably about that time that I finally lost my virginity, after a particularly drunken party with a strapping ballet dancer. I remember having to unbutton endless corsets and her being very understanding – I was 19 and very inexperienced!

Tim Morris was an incredible party animal and he managed to find a band for our twice-weekly parties – they needed somewhere to practise – and a constant flow of pretty girls. Unfortunately and inevitably the neighbour, a diplomat who had been extremely tolerant for several weeks, started complaining about the noise and rowdiness and we were forced to look elsewhere for somewhere to live.

I was lucky enough to be invited to share a mews flat with Peter Kearon, who worked for Knight Frank and Rutley. He was an extremely sophisticated and charming character, some three or four years my senior. The flat was in Queens Gate Mews and stretched my meagre budget to the limit, although I had passed my intermediate exam by that time, taking my weekly wage from £2 per week to £3. Peter Kearon also liked his parties, and soon after I moved in he gave a Mexican party where a friend of his, Alexander Plunkett Green (subsequently married to Mary Quant) painted a series of Mexican murals on the flat walls. Peter was a very generous and tolerant flatmate, but I couldn't really afford the rent and other outgoings.

At that time I had joined the Café de Paris Guinea Pig Club. This had been started by a certain Baron Teo Von Roth, a Hungarian, to encourage the younger generation to go to the Café. It was available only if you were under 25, and meant we could have dinner and a half bottle of wine for a guinea (21 shillings) a head. An amazing incentive! This was a very good deal for an impoverished student such as myself; it was such a bargain that I was able to propose a number of my friends to the club. One of those I introduced was Gawaine Baillie, who was at that time at Trinity College studying engineering and who became a great friend. Some time later I discovered that his mother owned Leeds Castle in Kent and that he was a baronet, his father having died when he was 17.

Gawaine Baillie, 1958

One evening we went to see Marlene Dietrich at the Café de Paris. It was an amazing evening – our table was on the balcony and I had invited two very pretty girls from Kent to come with us, one of whom I remember was Sally Eden. Marlene came down the stairs wearing a tight-fitting brilliant sequined dress, looking absolutely fabulous and incredibly beautiful – I suppose she must have been in her late 40s at that time. After being introduced by Nöel Coward, she sang in a wonderful deep voice. I remember the evening as if it were yesterday, although it is now over 50 years ago.

It must have been 1954 when I was invited to stay at Leeds Castle. Naively I had thought Leeds was in Yorkshire, and was rather surprised to find us being driven south into Kent in Gawaine's 1938 Bentley. He had been given a pipe of port as a christening present by one of his godparents and had sold it and bought the Bentley with the proceeds!

When we arrived I found we were part of a very large weekend party with a number of Cabinet Ministers and members of the Upper House, notably Duncan Sandys, Geoffrey Lloyd, David Margesson, the Duke and Duchess of Argyll and Prince and Princess (Grace) Radziwill, then the wife of Stas (before he married Lee Bouvier – Jackie Kennedy's sister) and the widow of an American senator. Our hostess, Lady Olive Baillie, was the sister of Dorothy Padget, the daughter of Lord Queensborough, and had been married to a couple of American millionaires before marrying Sir Adrian Baillie, Gawaine's father.

Olive Baillie was an attractive and highly intelligent lady with piercing blue eyes and an extremely dominant personality. She was very active politically behind the scenes and constantly entertained Cabinet Ministers at weekends, David Margesson being a frequent weekend visitor as he was then Government Chief Whip. Olive had bought the castle, one of Henry VIII's shooting lodges, with her sister Dorothy Paget in the late 1920s and had had it renovated with great flair and attention to detail.

Because of the large number of people staying, I was put in the old nursery wing of the castle with a wonderful view over the lake behind the castle and part of the moat. The most embarrassing moment came when the butler insisted on unpacking my case and laying out my clothes. I only had one dress shirt and my dressing gown was tatty and frayed – a hand-me-down from my elder brother.

The butler summoned us for dinner, which was preceded by drinks served in the white and gold library. I had never seen anything quite so elegant in my life before. At dinner – a magnificent six course event – there was a uniformed footman behind every chair. It was quite difficult to decide which knife and fork to use with each course, so I waited until my neighbour picked up theirs so that I could follow suit. After the first course I realised that all I had to do was start from the outside and progressively work my way in.

After dinner most of the party went to play bridge and backgammon. Having been warned that the stakes would be high, I wisely resisted. Unfortunately I was caught the next day playing croquet, where the stakes were more modest. I was doing quite well, even though I hadn't played much before, until I was asked to change partners and to partner Grace Radziwill, who was a seriously poor player. As a result I finished up losing almost £5 – all the cash I had brought down to tip the butler. For me it was an absolute catastrophe. It meant I was unable to leave a tip when I left on Sunday evening after dinner.

On Saturday evening, because there were 13 of us, a separate table had been set for Gawaine, his godfather, David Margesson, and me. During the dinner I was subjected to detailed questioning as to my origins, education, parentage and beliefs, my financial status and whether I owned the flat I lived in at Queens Gate Mews. I had to admit I only rented it. I'm not sure I passed muster, as I was only asked to stay at Leeds one more time afterwards. Perhaps it was the lack of the tip for the butler!

At that time I had not appreciated that such wealth existed in post-war Britain: it was a real eye-opener. Before that, the greatest luxury I had enjoyed was staying with my Great Aunt Laura with a cook/housekeeper and chauffeur, a couple of maids and gardeners. This had appeared to me the height of luxury. It made me realise that I was going to have to be very lucky and work very hard if I was ever to enjoy the standard of living of my parents, let alone my Great Aunt Laura. However, it also made me appreciate how lucky I was to be a member of a large family with devoted and loving parents and the great gift of good health.

One thing the weekend brought home to me was the difficult relationship between Olive Baillie and her son Gawaine. One day after lunch the butler brought an envelope to Gawaine on a silver tray. He had been summoned to see his mother in her study at three o'clock that day. Afterwards I asked him whether he had a problem. Although I didn't appreciate it at the time, being an only child was extremely difficult for him, although he did have older stepsisters. His mother also owned a magnificent town house in Lowndes Place, just off Belgrave Square, with some wonderful impressionist paintings, including at least one Renoir. It was where Gawaine used to stay when he was in London and when his mother was out of town.

In my last couple of years at Cassleton Elliott I had to work for several weeks at Holloway Bros, a major building company whose offices were close to the Tate Gallery. Most days I spent at least half an hour there trying to educate myself on impressionist art.

When visiting their clients in the West End I used to have lunch at the Grafton Street coffee house just off Dover Street with a number of party-going friends, notably Kipper Fisher and Nigel Dempster (who subsequently would work for Johnny Kimberley's PR company and become the Daily Mail diarist). Discussion over lunch concerned who had been at the last party, where the next one was going to be and how easy was it going to be to gatecrash – not that I ever did. At that time a number of upwardly-mobile debs' mothers did not know half the male escorts, relying on a list of suitable young men to invite, so they were often unaware of the odd gatecrasher. By comparison the girls tended to be rather excited to have a 'black sheep' at the party!

Johnny Kimberley and Janey, his sixth Countess

While living at Ely we had earlier attended point-to-point meetings at Cottenham and Fakenham, where one of the more successful riders was Johnny Kimberley on his horse Dick the Gee. Some years later we met again at the annual Liberal Party ball, where we had been invited by Rollo Denbigh to share a table with Johnny, both of whom had taken the

Liberal whip in the Lords. Rollo Denbigh was with his wife Judy, to whom I had introduced him at one of my parties, and Johnny was with an old friend, Janey Consett, later to become his sixth Countess, much against her wishes! They were a wonderful couple and over the years we enjoyed many shooting and fishing trips with them.

Sadly Johnny had lost his father in a bombing raid in London when he was only 16, when he had inherited the Earldom, a barony and one of the oldest baronetcies. His godfather was Sir Winston Churchill, and King George VI and Queen Elizabeth were present at his wedding in 1945 to Diana Leigh, daughter of Sir Piers Leigh, Master of the Royal Household.

Johnny had inherited ancestral Kimberly Hall, with its 5,000 acres. He had also inherited massive death duty liabilities as a result of both his father's and grandfather's early deaths, resulting in serious financial problems for a 21-year-old. He was then pressured by his mother to make a suitable marriage. When asked about his first marriage he told me that as he walked down the aisle at St George's Chapel, Windsor Castle, with the royal family in attendance, for the wedding to Diana he realised he was making a big mistake, but had to go through with it. In the event it turned out to be a disaster, she wanting the St. James's Palace life style and he loving the country.

Consequently a couple of years later he wanted a divorce, but needed to get the King's consent. According to Johnny the account of the discussion was as follows:

"W-w-why on earth do you w-w-w-want a divorce?" asked the King.

"Unfortunately we are not very suited and I don't love her."

"If you get a divorce you know you w-w-won't be able to come to shoot with me at Sandringham or go to A-A-Ascot and I won't be able to come and shoot with you at K-K-Kimberley. You will be ostracised from society. Do you want to g-g-give all that up?"

"I don't love her" said Johnny.

"W-W-What's love got to do with marriage?" asked the King. "Why don't you do like the rest of us?"

"What is that sir?" asked Johnny.

"Why not take a m-m-mistress?" replied the King.

Much easier to get rid of than wives!

One of the nightspots we patronised at that time was Al Burnett's Cabaret Club in Swallow Street. Burnett was a great comedian and orchestrated a number of acts. Any unaccompanied men were immediately provided with an attractive hostess. In exchange you had to buy them champagne at extortionate prices!

On one occasion I had been chatting up a particularly attractive hostess who told me she was an actress, but out of work. Quite attracted by her, I asked her whether she would like to come out after the show. She told me that the rules of the club did not allow the hostesses to leave at the same time as the guests.

I thought no more about it, but when Gawaine and I got back to Lowndes Place I was amazed to see a taxi drawing up behind ours with this lovely girl aboard. I had no alternative but to take her back to the flat in Queens Gate Mews for a ten-minute chat and then get her a taxi back home. Nobody believed me when I told them that it was all totally innocent. Life is full of so many missed opportunities!

Living in London at that time was most enjoyable. There was an extreme shortage of eligible bachelors, so any reasonably presentable young man with good manners owning a dinner jacket was generally accorded a warm welcome by London hostesses anxious for their daughters to meet the titled and well-heeled gentry. My friendship with Gawaine Baillie was a considerable advantage in the social stakes!

When I was 20 I moved into Scarsdale Villas to share two rooms in the top of the house with Roland Raemaker, an old school friend who was studying medicine. We were looked after as paying guests by the wife of the owner, who cooked us both breakfast and dinner. Most weekends were spent at my parents' home in Ely, where after a number of catering difficulties my parents had persuaded the RAF to replace the two batmen who helped run the house with 'batwomen' (more about them later), whom my mother found easier to organise and supervise. This helped to relieve pressure at the weekend, when there was always a full house and I was able to bring friends to stay and repay hospitality received from them.

Lifts to and from London came from Gawaine Baillie and Anthony Buck. In later years Anthony Buck became a Junior Defence Minister and his wife was involved in a scandal when she had an affair with the Chief of Defence staff, Sir Anthony Harding, who had to resign as a result.

The house in Ely was a very relaxed place. Before taking my accountancy exams I was able to spend four or five weeks revising in idyllic surroundings, walking and playing tennis to relieve the tedium of study. Fortunately, or unfortunately, this was not the only relief provided! The two batgirls were a very attractive and sexy pair, one full of jokes and fun, the other quiet and demure. They must have been in their late teens or early twenties. I will call them Jane and Betty.

My brothers and I were always joking and laughing with Jane, to the extent that when my mother went out shopping she would never leave her alone with me, as she was clearly anxious that my studies should not be disturbed. It was a serious mistake, because she always left the other one at home – Betty, the quiet one. Directly my mother left the house Betty would drag me upstairs and relieve the tensions of study in a most delightful way. On one occasion, when my father returned from his office at the hospital half an hour earlier than usual, she had to hide in a cupboard in my bedroom – an anxious moment, but not half as anxious as when several weeks later she telephoned to tell me that she thought she might be pregnant. Luckily it turned out to be a false alarm, but there were two or three days of anxiety and panic at the potential family shame. However, it was a valuable warning.

My parents had organised a 21st birthday party for me in Ely, to which I had invited 20 assorted friends from London, including Gawaine Baillie, Beverley Roberts, Tim Morris and Michael Shurey.

Beverley Roberts

Beverley was quite the most attractive and glamorous of my friends. In the later stages of the party she decided she "had to kiss the birthday boy" - who was nowhere to be found. A search party was dispatched to find me. When they did – to my horror – my brothers Charles and John decided that I was to be debagged. Very degrading on one's 21st birthday. I did not find the experience very amusing and fought off my tormentors with a vengeance – mind you it was a near thing!

Nevertheless it was a great party. We played tennis and cricket the next day and went rat shooting in the afternoon in some nearby barns, which had seen a rather different sort of action the night before. I can't remember where all the guests slept, no doubt some on the floor and some with local friends.

In 1954 I moved out of Scarsdale Villas into a house in the Little Boltons, where Jeremy Monson also rented a flat, as a tenant of Peter Parkinson.

Some months later, just before taking my final examination, I met a most amazing girl at a fancy dress party in Queens Gate. I had been lent an extremely ornate 18th century guards dress uniform belonging to Lord Monson, Jeremy's grandfather. It had gold epaulettes and gold braid everywhere. Despite my uneven teeth, I thought I looked amazing. On arrival at the party I was immediately transfixed by a gorgeous Puss in Boots – fishnet stockings coming up to her armpits, wonderful black hair. She was tall, with bright and flashing eyes and the most realistic whiskers, and had a luscious wide and inviting smile. Her name was Mary. It was lust at first sight.

The evening passed like a dream. We both drank an enormous amount of champagne and ended up in her flat in Hyde Park Gate, just round the corner not far away from the party. I walked back to the Little Boltons early in the morning full of the joys of spring, returning to Ely for the final weeks of study before my final exams. I was just 22.

CHAPTER 5

A DIVORCE FORETOLD
1955-8

What is life? 'Tis not hereafter
Present mirth hath present laughter
What's to come is still unsure
In delay there lies no plenty
So come kiss me, sweet-and-twenty
Youth's the stuff will not endure.
- Shakespeare

During my first few years of articles, work experience had been repetitive and boring. I had to add up long lists of figures and post hundreds of journal entries from one ledger to another. Later years included the examination of accounting systems, control methods and taxation. All in all I found the technical side of accountancy less interesting than the business activities involved. I consequently decided to leave the accounting profession and go into industry at the earliest possible opportunity.

The advice I received from the profession was that four extra years working for a firm of chartered accountants would help my career, rather than going into industry straight away. Having been turned down on health grounds (as a result of the pneumonia as a child), I was unable to do my National Service with the Irish Guards as I had hoped. I rejected the offer of an immediate commission in the Pay Corps and was luckily not required to complete the two years of National Service in the army. It was a great relief.

I took the finals of the chartered accountancy examination in May 1955. Probably as a result of the time I had spent revising in Ely and some extra tuition, I scraped through on my first attempt, when only 43% of those taking the exam passed.

Not having to do my National Service gave me an unexpected bonus of two years. Accordingly I signed up to join Peat Marwick Mitchell in their Paris office so that I could spend time in another country and hopefully learn a foreign language – something which I had singularly failed to do at Stonyhurst. Working in Paris also provided valuable experience of a different approach to financial control and different accountancy methods. In Paris, Peat Marwick Mitchell were employed, among other responsibilities, to audit and verify the accounts of the subsidiaries of American and British multinationals. The emphasis was on ensuring that the assets and liabilities these companies showed in their accounts actually existed. I'd been told that most French companies kept two sets of books – if they did, I never found the extra set!

Paris in 1956 was a very exciting place compared to the rather drab post-war London. However rented accommodation was very difficult to find and most of the properties which were available for rental were unfurnished.

Marriage at 22 had not been part of my game plan, but the fancy dress party had been my undoing and with a daughter on the way I had just got married to Mary, my Puss in Boots. This posed a serious financial problem, particularly as I had not told my parents of the wedding, which had taken place at Kensington register office with Gawaine Baillie as my best man, followed by a lunch at the Caprice, just behind the Ritz.

In those days public opinion was such that with the birth of our daughter, Joanna, it was no bad thing that we lived the first eighteen months of married life abroad.

During our early days of marriage, apart from house hunting, we visited all the museums and art galleries and took long walks along the banks of the Seine, hunting through the various riverside stalls selling pictures, prints and tourist trinkets.

After one such morning we were waiting to have lunch in a cheap and cheerful restaurant close to the Louvre just off the Avenue de l'Opera. While we were waiting for a table to become free I noticed an old gypsy fortune teller reading the hands of some of the other lunchers. As we had several minutes to wait we decided to have our fortunes told (despite it costing 50 francs each).

I was the first to put my hand out to be read. She looked at my hand for several minutes and then told me that I would travel a lot during my life and that one day I would become rich. It would not be through inheritance, but all from my own efforts. Good news, I thought. She then looked at my hand again and continued that I would have three children, but that she could not tell me anything else.

Mary then asked her to read her hand. She looked at it for several minutes and then told her she was unable to do so! After a great deal of persuasion, at Mary's insistence, she told her she would travel a lot and live most of her life in foreign lands away from her country of birth. She went on to say that she would have one child. At this, Mary protested that the fortune teller had just told me that I would have three children, so how could that be right? The fortune teller protested that she could only tell her what was in her hand.

Although this all happened over 50 years ago, I can still remember it as though it was yesterday. Everything the fortune teller read in our hands came true, an extraordinary outcome. I did have to wait a very long time before I considered myself to be the slightest bit rich, but I certainly didn't inherit anything much.

It seems incredible to me that some gifted individuals should be able to forecast with such accuracy from merely reading a hand. It may well be that the fortune teller also saw in Mary's hand something that she did not want to reveal. How could she have forecast that she would only have one child and live most of her life abroad?

After about a year of living and working in Paris, Mary, who had not learned a great deal of French, wanted to go back to England. As a result we returned to London, where we were constantly at loggerheads. It culminated in an argument when hanging curtains in a newly-rented apartment in Kensington Church Street, one that I've regretted ever since. During the argument she started to punch and kick me. In an attempt to restrain her I gripped her wrists, holding her away from me until she stopped. When she stopped I let her go, but as she walked past me she turned round and punched me hard on the side of the head. Unfortunately, I saw red and retaliated. With considerable abuse, she departed down the road to her parents' flat in Iverna Court.

An hour or two later her father appeared to tell me she wanted a divorce. We had been married no longer than two years. Not a happy state of affairs.

After we parted a couple of years later she met her second husband and went to live abroad, first in Malta and then in the South of Spain, where she now lives with a female partner - was this the reason the fortune teller initially refused to read her hand?

I could not afford to remain in the flat on my own, so I moved into a rather dingy maisonette in Kensington Church Street as a paying guest at a weekly rental of £4 per week, just under half the rent we had been paying on the flat. The flat was above an antique shop at the top of Kensington Church Street and consisted of a large sitting room, adjacent kitchen with two bedrooms and a bathroom on the landing between the floors. I accepted the smaller back bedroom, as it was quieter, and immediately set about redecorating it.

The tenant was a very charming producer with the BBC. Very soon after, he decided to get married and moved out, transferring the tenancy to me. I was then able to invite David Wingfield, a good friend, to share the flat with me. This was an inspired choice, as we were of a similar age with a liking for parties, and we both enjoyed a touch of colour in our separate lives. David was also an extremely good cook and had an excellent memory for names.

Despite the grotty state of the flat we settled down to party and enjoy the London social life. We gave frequent dinner parties, and I became adept at setting the table and washing up afterwards while David performed in the kitchen.

110A Kensington Church Street became a legendary place for late night parties. From time to time we were fortunate enough to persuade band leader Comfrey Philips to bring some of his band to play at the flat. Luckily the floors above the adjoining antique shops were not occupied during the evenings, so we did not have much trouble with the neighbours!

David's elder brother lived on his estate in Gloucestershire and had four daughters. As the estate was entailed it could only pass to a male heir, so at that time David was the heir to Barrington Park and 6000 acres in the best part of Gloucestershire. He was consequently much in demand by London society hostesses. Rumours of wild parties at 110a, whilst enhancing our reputation with the girls, did not go down too well with the hostesses. Nor did my divorce!

At that time I met a really lovely girl, Lee Fisher, whose father was mayor of Kensington and who lived with her parents, or rather her father and stepmother, just off Gloucester Road. She was blonde, tall and elegant and was running her father's motor business in Earls Court (A-1 Garage). It was through her that I acquired my first motorcar. I only took out girls within ten minutes' walking distance of Kensington Church Street, as I couldn't afford too many taxi fares, so the acquisition of a motorcar was a step in the right direction.

We had a sweet relationship, more like brother and sister, nothing more serious. Not surprisingly, her father did not approve. Not only was I a Catholic, but I was divorced – in those days, a contradiction in terms. Nor did I have any money, and I had a dependant daughter (which although a major incentive to succeed, certainly didn't help with potential new parents-in-law).

The parties at 110A became a regular feature, with a succession of friends and other hangers-on together with many different characters. This included not only the smart set, but also the flotsam and jetsam of Chelsea society. There were a number of notorious characters, including Bobby Buchanan Michaelson, whose main claim to fame was to have taken Princess Elizabeth and Princess Margaret to the Old 400 Club in Leicester Square after a debutante's party - that is, until he took the rap for exporting copper to Russia, which was embargoed at that time. I was told that Stephen Ward once brought Christine Keeler to 110A: if he did, I can't remember it. One of the drinks to be consumed at our parties was Merrydown cider, which was approximately 20% proof and specially directed to those visitors who didn't want anything too alcoholic!

Gambling was still illegal in the fifties and we saw the growth of illegal gambling parties in private houses in Chelsea, Kensington and Knightsbridge. In order to avoid detection a different venue was used every time. I had been to a few of these parties, mainly as an observer. Sometimes I had a few chips on the roulette table, occasionally winning but more often losing. On one occasion the party in Lennox Gardens was short of a banker and I foolishly offered to take the bank, unusually having about £25 on me – quite a lot in those days.

To start with it went extremely well and after an hour or so I was up £250. It was then 11.30 pm, but at 12 o'clock there were new arrivals. To my horror, they backed and surrounded number 17, which won twice!

I was in deep trouble, the £250 gain having turned into a £500 loss. I was sweating heavily, and it took me until ten past two to recover most, but not all, of the loss.

I didn't take the bank again, but I did have a brief walk out with the party organiser a year later in St Tropez. This happened on holiday in Cannes when I had driven down to the South of France with three girls who were helping me to pay for the petrol – they were past, present and future girlfriends. By the time we arrived in Cannes, after a lot of chatter, the present and the future one had both become past as well. So I drove along to St Tropez alone. I had booked into a local hotel and was twiddling my thumbs in one of the harbour cafés when I ran into Jenny, the owner of the apartment where the party had taken place. She needed a bed for the night and next day a lift down the coast to meet up with a girlfriend of hers with an enormous flat. Unfortunately, despite the size of the flat and the enormous bedroom, there was only one bed, measuring about nine feet by seven – incredible! I had never been in such a big bed before in my life. Unfortunately three of us had to share it. Not knowing which way to turn, I finished up in the bathroom trying to get some sleep on my own. As I said before, life is full of missed opportunities!

David and I had a wide circle of friends and in the early 1960s we got involved in throwing a rather unusual party on an underground train on the Circle Line. We started from Sloane Square wth a band, a case of champagne and two dozen glasses. More partygoers got on at Gloucester Road and it got increasingly rowdy until we baled out at Notting Hill Gate, to continue the party at 110A. There was quite a fuss in the Evening Standard the next day. Luckily my name was not mentioned, as it might have damaged my prospects at GEC. After that I was very careful to keep my private life and business activities completely separate, particularly when I was at LWT.

CHAPTER 6

SPANISH INTERLUDE
1959-1961

In 1959 and 1960 I took a number of holidays in the south of Spain. The first was in 1959, when I rented a villa in Mijas for four weeks. It was a lovely four-bedroom house with a large garden and swimming pool called Huerta Alta ("high orchard"), and at that time it was one of only two houses in the village owned by Brits. It came with a cook and gardener and the rental was ten pounds per week.

I drove down with a girlfriend in a new car and had a number of chums to stay each week. The road from the coast to the house was at that time little more than a dirt track with precipitous drops on either side of the road. As the crow flies the house was probably only two miles from the sea, but by the hazardous road it was approximately eight miles.

We used to stay by the pool most of the day and descend to the coast in the late afternoon to swim, drink, dive and dance, driving back in the early hours of the morning at breathtaking speed up the hill.

My girlfriend at the time was Mary Rose Donaldson from the South African mining family, whose first action each morning was to pour herself a large vodka and tonic. Her grandfather had been a partner of Cecil Rhodes but had parted company with Rhodes when he had decided to explore what was to become Rhodesia. Mary Rose was a wayward but extremely amusing and entertaining character who used to take full advantage of the abundance of

Trying my hand in the bullring in Spain, 1962

Dancing with Mary-Rose Donaldson in southern Spain, 1962

cheap alcohol which was then available in Southern Spain. A large Fundador bandy cost the equivalent of 2½ pence and she used to say you could get drunk for two and six.

Mary Rose had a twin brother who went off to fight in the Congo but never came back. His father arranged a search party and eventually found some burned out remains; apparently he had been killed and eaten – a tragic loss for the family.

Some years later, after a couple of failed marriages, Mary Rose ended up severely ill in Sardinia, I think of cirrhosis of the liver. She died at the age of 35, soon after being brought back to the UK by her first husband, Jeremy Renton, a wealthy stockbroker who rather enjoyed the bohemian life in Chelsea.

Soon afterwards one of my friends, Michael Shurey, having lost money he didn't have gambling on the stock market, was bailed out by his father (not for the first time) on condition he went abroad for at least two years, either to Australia or South Africa. He chose South Africa and on arrival in Johannesburg was invited to stay the weekend with the Donaldsons. He stayed not just for a weekend but for two years, being treated as a surrogate son, much to Mary Rose's irritation. He was a very entertaining character. Subsequently he came good selling Mills and Boon books in South Africa.

One of our guests was so petrified by the way I drove back from the coast in the evening that the next day he insisted on driving himself in his hire car. Mary Rose and I were happy to be his passengers. Not being used to the practice of taking corners on loose gravel, halfway up the hill he drove his rented car into a ditch on a hairpin bend. Fortunately it was on the mountain side of the road - on the other side of the road there was a thirty-foot ft drop. It would not have been at all amusing.

We had all drunk far too much that evening and we were terrified that the local police would find us and lock us in jail. We started bumping the car up and down, putting stones in the ditch under the tyres, and after an exhausting two hours we were able to bounce the car out of the ditch and back on to the road. We arrived back at the villa in the morning light rather more sober than we started out.

This was an extremely interesting trip, on which I met a number of characters and very nearly started a property company. The individual who was due to provide the capital to finance the company was just out of the army with a golden bonus. Unfortunately he disappeared off to Germany in pursuit of a flaxen-haired nymphet, and the project collapsed.

About that time David had a very attractive half-Indian girlfriend, Janet Aiyer – later to become the Countess of Cowley. She was a most exciting character with an amazing speaking voice, and a great enthusiast who brought life and excitement to 110a. Sadly the marriage to Dennis Cowley didn't last and she subsequently married the MP Piers Dixon. Dennis died soon afterwards of a heart attack in an escort's bedroom in Bayswater, possibly helped by sniffing too much ammonitrate. There was probably a genetic heart problem, as his son and heir died playing squash at the age of 27.

Some years later I was staying with John Wingfield, David's younger brother, who was running a car rental company in Fuengirola, and was chatting up a very pretty Danish air hostess called Josephine Plum on the beach. She had won the contest for air hostess of the year in 1958 and was on holiday with her very rich and fat mother, Madame Plum of the Plumrose family.

At that time I was working at GEC, which did not appear particularly glamorous, so when asked what I did for a living I told Josephine that I was a psychiatrist. This immediately seemed to excite her. Having a doctor as a father and with some superficial reading, I was able to comment on Jung and Pavlov with apparent authority. She appeared interested and insisted I should meet her mother – not quite what I had bargained for.

One morning we had been talking for about ten minutes when a Belgian lady, whose husband I had earlier helped to find a garage for his car, started to become very agitated. Her husband had swum out through a heavy surf and was waving frantically. She was sure he was drowning. "Not drowning, only waving", I said. "No, he is in serious trouble, go and rescue him" said Josephine. I couldn't refuse. I tore off through the surf with the heavy waves breaking over me and eventually reached the Belgian, who was in very poor shape and frothing at the mouth, but still afloat.

I had read enough about life saving to know that I had to put one arm around his neck and hold his head above the water. I swam using back strokes, using my legs and one free arm, towards the shore. It was going quite well, although he hadn't spoken a word, until we got to the surf, where the incoming waves met a strong undercurrent going out to sea. The waves were constantly breaking over both of us, and I was swallowing water.

Fortunately a fishing boat had been launched through the surf to pick us up. We managed to get the Belgian aboard and I was pulled out after him, totally exhausted. I put the Belgian on the floor of the boat, head down, and attempted to give him artificial respiration while the boatman brought the boat through the heavy surf. Unfortunately as he did so several big waves broke over the boat, which then started to fill with water, and I had to lift the Belgian's head out of the water, propping him up in a sitting position.

Fortunately the boat came through the surf and I started to shout for a doctor - "*Hoy necessito una medico por favour!*" When we got close to the shore I could hear Josephine saying to a number of onlookers that we already had a doctor on board – me - so there was no need for another. I had really been hoist by my own petard!

Luckily, when we got to the shore and lifted the Belgian out of the boat on to the beach, there was a real medico there, an Austrian, who took over. But despite attempted mouth-to-mouth resuscitation his efforts were to no avail and the man never regained consciousness. It really spoilt the holiday for us both.

Madame Plum gave a dinner several days later to thank both me and the Austrian doctor, who luckily didn't speak very good English, otherwise my cover as a psychiatrist would have been totally blown. However, I was extremely depressed by the event and have never pretended to be a psychiatrist again.

Subsequently my father asked me to give a detailed account of the event. He told me that the frothing at the mouth indicated to him that the Belgian had had a heart attack and I could not reproach myself for allowing him to drown. However it was a sobering experience and one which was only partially alleviated by a visit to the bullring several days later, when a number of us entered the ring with some young bulls. I still have the photos to remind me of that event.

CHAPTER 7

BAPTISM IN BUSINESS
1959–1963

On my return to the UK in 1957 I had joined Russell Tillett, a firm of chartered accountants which was occupying the same building as my soon-to-be-ex father-in-law. In 1959, following my divorce, I left Russell Tillett and joined GEC as assistant secretary.

Some two years earlier Arnold Weinstock and his father-in-law, Michael Sobel, had sold Radio and Allied Holdings to GEC for shares in GEC, obtaining seats on the board for themselves. The company secretary, Anthony Parsons, had been brought into the company to implement the restructuring of the company which had been recommended by consultants Urwick Orr & Co. A major proposal for the reorganisation had been the decentralisation of the company, which previously had seven divisions all trading through a dozen provincial branch offices in the UK.

My initial responsibilities included setting up an estates department, selling off the majority of the branch offices and finding smaller separate offices for the seven divisional trading companies. In the process I was appointed secretary to the newly-established electronics and telecommunications divisions of the company. With the new appointment I got a salary increase, which helped my lifestyle no end but still left me with relatively little surplus income.

I was really beginning to enjoy working at the head office in Magnet House, Kingsway (one of the properties GEC had decided to sell). We were in negotiation with a number of different developers, including Felix Fenston (who was in partnership with Stas Radziwill) to discuss the possible sale of Magnet House. Quite separately I had met his son Tim at a party and had been to dinner with him in Dolphin Square. When he found out I was involved in the sale of Magnet House he became even keener to develop our friendship, inviting me to go and shoot snipe and woodcock on the island of Islay in September that year.

Sadly shortage of funds prevented me from accepting the invitation. I was mortified that I was unable to go. In the event it was a fortunate decision, as the plane bringing Tim and his farm manager back to London on Tuesday morning crashed at Heathrow airport and tragically they were both killed, one of the very few accidents that have occurred at Heathrow. It was tragic for the family, in particular for Felix, as Tim was his blue-eyed boy, but it was an incredibly lucky escape for me. Had I not been so strapped financially I would have been on that plane.

A year or so later I was invited to the opening party of Lee House in London Wall, a development by Metropolitan Estates and Property Company, owned by Felix Fenston and Stas Radziwill and named after Stas' new wife, Lee Bouvier.

Stas brought Lee over to talk to me, as we had met at Leeds Castle some years earlier. At the time I was talking to Jack Cotton, a very successful property developer. Unfortunately Jack wanted to discuss the sale of one of GEC's properties, so after listening to

Lee Fisher

My parents with John Tolhurst (left)
at a family wedding

Best man at my brother John's wedding

us for ten minutes Lee made her excuses and left – another missed opportunity! When she had left I said to Jack that he had chased away the pretty lady. He remarked that that was unimportant. What mattered was the discussion we had been having. It was a lesson in priorities.

Felix and Tim were great pranksters, probably due to their Irish blood. Johnny K used to tell a number of stories about jokes they all played on each other. I remember one which concerned three legendary millionaires, Charlie Clore, Jack Cotton and Charlie Forte (subsequently Lord Forte), none of whom were noted for having loose purse strings. Through their secretaries, Felix arranged for the three to be invited to have lunch together at the Ritz, each thinking they had been invited by one of the others, with some expensive wines pre-ordered. Felix had reserved a table close by as he wanted to see what happened when the bill arrived. Apparently at first it was ignored, then the bill was pushed from one to the other several times before Felix stepped in to stop a furious argument and paid the bill.

After some two years working at GEC running the estates department and assisting Anthony Parsons and Ken Smith as company secretary, it appeared that Arnold Weinstock had initiated a number of further consultants' reports into the structure and management at GEC. The consultants recommended a wholesale change in the structure of both the board and the management of the company, a major coup for Arnold Weinstock, who I suspect had largely dictated the contents of the recommendations, assisted by the deputy chairman, T B O Kerr.

This resulted in the wholesale dismissal of the top echelon of the GEC board including the chairman and finance director, the financial controller and my boss, the company secretary. At that time I was 26 and having set up the property department under a newly-recruited manager, Courtney Young, I was assigned to the United Power Company (UPC), a consortium with contracts to build nuclear power stations at Hunterston and Tokai Mura in Japan. I was reporting to the newly-appointed finance director of GEC, Kenneth Bond (later Sir Kenneth).

I wasn't all that keen at the prospect, as I had lost a boss I liked and I could not see much valuable experience being gained in trying to control the costs of something as complex as a nuclear power station. However I agreed to do the job for two years on condition that I should receive a terminal bonus at the end of that period. The alternative would have been to leave GEC, which I thought might not look so good on my CV.

When running the property operation at GEC I had questioned the issue of 125-year leases, a longer lease costing double the rate of stamp duty than a 99-year lease. I proposed to Herbert Smith, GEC's solicitors, that instead of granting 125-year leases they should grant 99-year leases with mutual options by landlord and tenant to renew for a further 25 years, thus halving the stamp duty payable. After initial resistance and after taking counsel opinion, Herbert Smith reported that this was possible. Consequently long leases were subsequently agreed using this option, with considerable savings to GEC. Not that it reflected in my pay packet!

My social life at that time was pretty hectic. My parents had retired to Marlow, where I and my brothers were delighted to find that a finishing school for girls had been established and that a number of my parents' friends had very pretty daughters. Marlow then became a great place to spend weekends, particularly in summer – lots of parties and waterskiing.

In London there were also a number of bars and clubs we patronised, among them Esmeralda's Barn in Wilton Place, owned by the notorious Kray brothers, where Noel Harrison, Cy Grant and Lance Percival played their guitars, while Lance made up calypsos at the request of the guests. We also dined at the relatively cheap Italian restaurants San Lorenzo and San Frediano, going on to the Blue Angel in Berkeley Street and Helen Cordet's Saddle Room as well as the Garrison at the bottom of Park Lane. The Blue Angel frequently had floor shows with artists such as Leslie Hutchinson ('Hutch'), who appeared to enjoy being mobbed up, while Helen Cordet ran the Saddle Room with great charm and aplomb. One evening at Helen Cordet's with an old friend, Michael Whiting, we were joined by King Hussein of Jordan, who had been with him at Sandhurst.

At 110a we gave regular drinks parties and organised dinner afterwards, having previously booked a large table for dinner, with San Lorenzo being a favourite. After one late evening the owner told us he was too tired to give us a bill, so he charged us £5 per head

Josiane Buydance-Grimberg

– a really good deal in those days. We then took the party on to the Garrison, which had become a favourite, or, in later years, the Rascasse Club, where I had complimentary membership. We visited Annabel's from time to time, but it was not one of our favourites.

On one occasion I rather overdid the parties. I had been in London on Saturday night with a rather exciting lady, so did not get much sleep. The next day one of the French contingents from the finishing school flew into Heathrow, where I met her. She wanted to spend the afternoon at 110A in London before driving down to be delivered to Marlow Place, the finishing school, so when I drove back to London at 11.30 that evening I was quite tired. (This was before the M4 was built; the road back to London was the A40, which you joined at Wycombe).

A car I had been following suddenly turned right in front of me just as I was about to overtake. In an attempt to avoid it I ended up in a ditch, hitting my head and ending up in the local hospital with severe concussion. I could not remember what had happened or whether I was alone at the time of the accident.

The loss of memory persisted, with a blinding headache for a number of weeks until I was able to return to work. Some weeks later I tried to underplay the seriousness of the accident and refused to claim through the insurance company for personal injuries as I thought it might damage my career prospects and put up my insurance premiums.

One of the problems in the Tokai Mura project was that the quotation had been prepared prior to the finalisation of the detailed design of the reactor. As the site on which it was being built was close to a major volcanic fault line, the reactor had to be made earthquake proof. In particular the design for the loading and unloading of the radio-active reactor fuel - an extremely delicate operation - had not been completed before the estimate had been finalised. In the event the cost escalation on this piece of equipment amounted to some twenty times the amount of original estimate. Further problems in the construction of the power station arose from the steel supplied by the British supplier, Colvilles, which developed serious cracking after delivery and had to be totally replaced, causing serious delays.

At the outset I had told Kenneth Bond that it would be unlikely that I would be able to have much control over the financial outcome other than to inform GEC in advance of the likely cost overruns. Accordingly a significant part of the two years I spent on the project was preparing justification for cost increases and preparation for the claims against suppliers, in particular Colvilles. This required extensive negotiation with the Japanese operator.

On one occasion, after several days of detailed negotiations, I was asked to organise the entertainment of our Japanese guests. They had asked to be taken to a particular club in Beak Street, Soho. I knew it only by reputation, and it proved to be a rather sleazy club. Neither I nor Harry Klein, the project director, had ever been there before. Accordingly I became a member in the afternoon so that I was able to greet our Japanese guests on arrival at the club.

We were enjoying our first drink when the Japanese chief executive asked me how long I had been a member of the club, as I had been greeted extremely warmly on arrival. I diplomatically replied, "not very long". A few minutes later one of the hostesses, who I had not seen, put her hands over my face from behind and asked me to guess who she was. I had no idea! She turned out to be a very pretty girl I had often seen in Eaton Place, but had never met before. "We see you velly well known here" was the Japanese comment. After that the negotiations went much better!

The hostess turned out to be a girlfriend of the antique dealer Hog Dibbon, who lived at 21 Eaton Place, in the same building as one of my friends, Natasha Horlick. I had often seen her on the stairs, but never realised she earned her living as a hostess! Such was my naivety in those days.

I left GEC at the end of four years to join Staveley Industries, a substantial group of companies involved in the manufacture of machine tools, chemicals, foundries and abrasives and electrical contracting, reporting directly to the finance director with the extraordinary title of Group Financial Analysis Manager. In effect I was an internal management consultant.

The five years working at GEC proved to be more useful than I expected. The contract negotiations with the Japanese authorities and the methods of control and management of large construction contracts were invaluable. It also gave me experience in the inevitable conflicts which can arise in consortia companies with different commercial priorities as well as the London commercial property market.

CHAPTER 8

SWINGING THROUGH THE SIXTIES
1963-1969

Before starting the job with Staveley I arranged with Kenneth Bond a mutually-convenient date for my departure. I waited for my bonus to arrive so I could enjoy a four-week break between jobs. Unfortunately it required a solicitor's letter to prise out the promised bonus. GEC was always very careful with its cash; not so in later years under Lord Simpson.

My job at Staveley turned out to be that of troubleshooter and internal management consultant. It was one of the most interesting and rewarding jobs possible. Staveley Industries was the rump of a nationalised steel company, chaired by ex-civil servant Dennis Havilland, who had decided to modernise the UK machine tool industry through a programme of acquisitions and consolidation, most of which subsequently proved to be ill-judged. My early years at Staveley were spent within the chemicals division in modernising lime kilns in Derbyshire and replacing Staveley's outdated salt works with a brand-new factory in consortiums with Cerebos at Sandbach to create British Salt. The new salt works turned out to be an extremely efficient and profitable operation.

In subsequent years my job involved the merging and closure of a number of machine tool manufacturers in the Manchester area, the largest being Craven Bros. and Kendall and Gent. At that time there was extreme pressure of competition from German and Japanese manufacturers, with the replacement of conventional machine tools by automated computer controlled machine tools. The job involved extensive travel and entitled me to a company car.

The ten years from 1959 to 1969 included a lot of hard work and an active social life, with weekdays in London and weekends in Marlow, often with my daughter Joanna, who was growing up to be a very beautiful young lady. There were a number of prominent families living in the Marlow area, notably the Abercassis, the Martin Bates, the Hambledons, the Norfolks and the Kidds, a number of them with very pretty daughters. And of course there was the aforementioned finishing school, Marlow Place, filled with a succession of exotic foreign girls, most of whom were more mature than their English counterparts. We consequently had a very busy social life with a constant round of parties at the weekends. My brothers and I were spoilt for choice, although I, as a divorcee with a young daughter, was naturally regarded with considerable reservation.

In those days I took out a number of different girls both in London and in the country, including Lee Fisher, whose father, as previously mentioned, was the Mayor of Kensington and who, in addition to owning a garage in Earls Court, had an estate in Cumberland with salmon fishing on the River Derwent.

About the same time I met Vivian, the incredibly beautiful daughter of one of my parents' friends, who had just returned from a finishing school in Paris. Unknown to her parents she had taken off to Corsica for a couple of wild weeks, where she and two friends had a whale of a time with the local Corsican fishermen. She was not over enthusiastic at the prospect of spending summer in dull Marlow, and was quite excited by the idea of a divorcee of 29 with a flat in London. Not surprisingly, her parents were less enthusiastic!

When she was just 18 she asked me to take her to a local beauty contest. Against my better judgement, I did so. Not surprisingly she won it, as she really had the most beautiful face and figure. Soon afterwards she invited me to her grandfather's house, as they were away on holiday, a seductive invitation. She really had the most exciting and delightful body!

We had a wonderful clandestine affair for several months, with frequent trips to London and the occasional visit to her father's boat, which was moored in a quiet spot on the Thames at Marlow. We also went waterskiing in one of the local gravel pits and walking in Marlow Woods.

And then, a couple of months into the affair, I received a distraught telephone call from Vivian to tell me her mother had found her diary under the mattress in her bedroom.

"So what?" I asked,

"But I had put everything in it!" she said.

"Surely not everything?"

"Everything!"

"Deny it all."

"Too late!"

She had confessed everything to her parents, who wanted to see me at 10 o'clock on Saturday, in two days' time. I duly arrived at 10 am in my pale blue MGB, spraying the pebbles from the drive on to the lawn, to be greeted by a very red-faced and irate father and a very subdued Vivian.

"I understand you have been having an affair with my daughter!" he said. "I want to know what you're going to do about it! You have been a frequent guest in this house, your parents are friends and I believe you have abused our hospitality. Are you going to marry my daughter? If not I don't want you to see her ever again. If you do, I will make her a ward of court."

"We have only been going out for a few weeks" I said. "Isn't it a bit premature to think about marriage?" I went on to say that I couldn't understand what all the fuss was about. Had she been pregnant or had I been the first one, I could understand his anger.

I then realised they hadn't read the whole diary but only the last few weeks, which did not include the trip to Corsica. At that his face turned purple.

"That is the most disgusting thing I've heard today. Well, I want to know whether you're going to marry my daughter or not!"

I replied that marriage was a very important commitment and was not something that could be dealt with in five minutes and which Vivian and I had never discussed.

"Well, discuss it now!" he said.

I replied "Surely you don't expect us to discuss such an important matter with you present?"

"All right" he said, "I'll leave the room. I give you ten minutes".

When he left I turned to the lovely Vivian, who was looking subdued and lonely. My heart went out to her. "Your parents have gone over the top and are out for our blood. How are we going to deal with it?" I asked.

"I leave it to you" she replied.

"Okay" I said, "there is only one thing for it. We will tell them that we are getting engaged. You can also tell them that I have no money, I have a coloured girlfriend in London [not strictly true, but it helped the story] and a large overdraft. That will really put them off. We will have taken the wind out of their sails and they will very soon change their minds. How about that as an idea?"

When her father returned he asked what we had decided.

"We are engaged" I replied.

"What does that exactly mean?"

"I thought it meant that we would be getting married" I replied.

"When?" he asked (it was September).

"What about May next year?" I suggested. "This will give your wife plenty of time to make the arrangements."

"Not soon enough" he said.

He then poured himself a large Scotch whisky. "I suppose I have to congratulate you then" he said, pouring one out for me with some reluctance.

"I don't drink spirits" I said.

I left after arranging to pick Vivian up later to go to a drinks party with a family called Warneford-Davies, before going on to a party which was being given by my parents for my sister Maryanne's 21st.

At 5.30 pm I received a telephone call from Vivian in tears, to say that her mother had cut up all her dresses and locked her in her bedroom. Poor girl! I told her to climb out of her window and I would pick her up in a lane at the back of the house. Unfortunately she didn't have the heart to do so, with all her dresses in ribbons.

The following day I brought back to their house some glasses my parents had borrowed for my sister's party and was met by the irate father. He asked me whether I had told my parents of the engagement. The answer being 'no', he forbade me from seeing Vivian again, with the threat of a court order if I tried to do so. He told me he would not be prepared to allow the friendship to continue unless we were married immediately. I drove away feeling very sorry for Vivian, but with a great sense of relief that the strategy had worked. I was not ready to re-marry! Partying in London and Marlow continued apace.

In 1967 I bought my first property, a 16th century cottage in the little hamlet of Skirmett, near Henley. It belonged to an old lady called Vera Batt and was privately on the market. It had been a pub a century earlier and was in a dreadful state.

A local builder had offered Mrs Batt £3500 for it. The only way I could secure the property was by promising to equal the offer, with an immediate payment of 10% in cash. Accordingly I telephoned my solicitor and despite his warnings as to the question of title, he gave me a form of words to be included in a paper for her signature, which, next day, she signed on receipt of a deposit of £350 in cash, to the outrage of the builder and his solicitor.

Almost every weekend for the next two years was occupied with modernising and decorating the cottage. I was soon running out of cash, despite securing a £4000 mortgage. Getting a company car from Staveley allowed me to sell the love of my life, the souped-up MGB, for £850 and finish the work on the cottage. It was a very sad parting, but it was a great move forward to have a smart company car – a Sunbeam Rapier – with all the costs reimbursed.

Despite carrying out a senior management function, I was not being paid what I felt I was worth and could see the incredible waste of Staveley's massive investment in trying to save the machine tool industry. It was time to move on.

In 1968 I applied to an advertisement for the post of Finance Director Designate in a company called Modern Telephones, a publicly-quoted telephone rental company. The chief executive, a chartered accountant, was about to retire, to be succeeded by the current finance director. On the face of it, it appeared to be a thriving company with strong profitability; an attractive opportunity for me to get on to the board of a quoted company. It also offered a much better salary than I was being paid at Staveley.

After securing the job and following advice from a city friend, I started to look more closely into the company's accounts. It appeared that in order to sustain the profitability of the company, significant new capital had to be raised each year. I then started to analyse the basis on which profits were brought to account. Typically this involved rental contracts for a period of ten years. These were valued on a DCF basis (discounted cash flow) of the future rental receipts after allowance for maintenance costs of 20%. Further analysis showed me that over a ten-year contract this typically brought to account the majority of the profit on each contract in the early years, with a small percentage falling in the final years. However in order to sustain the profit level, significant extra capital had to be borrowed each year.

When account was taken of the interest cost on the borrowed capital the level of profit taken in the first four years of each contract amounted to some 140% of the total contract profit, with an estimated loss of 40% in the final six years. Having checked and re-checked the figures (bearing in mind there were already five qualified chartered accountants employed by the company), and made allowance for contract extensions and early cancellations, maintenance costs, etc, I had an extremely difficult meeting with the finance director, where I identified the weakness in the basis for the contract valuations, which, in my view, had clearly overstated profit for a number of years.

I advised both him and the chief executive that I would be unable to accept the job as finance director and would be looking for another job. Not a happy situation. It is interesting to note that both the chief executive and finance director resigned very soon afterwards.

Earlier that year I made my first skiing trip to Lech in Austria with an old friend, Lawrence Lamport, a very experienced skier who had been trying to get me on the slopes for a number of years. We drove out in my company car to join a large UK party organised by Simon Green, who put together skiing parties of between fifteen and twenty. Although I'm sure he did not make a profit, I suspect he and his wife got a free trip as a result. Before the holiday, encouraged by Lawrence, I went off to the artificial ski slope in Ruislip for several hours' practice.

When we arrived in Lech we found the roads to the resort had only just been cleared of snow and it was still piled up round our hotel, the Hotel Elizabeth, a four-star hotel on the edge of town.

The party was predominantly men of my age with a sprinkling of sporting girls. I was amazed to see the wonderful winter landscape and to experience the crisp sunny weather. Why had I left it so long?

Next morning Lawrence insisted we take a chairlift to the top of the slopes. After trying to follow him – I fell most of the way down – I took myself off to the nursery slopes, where I succeeded in going from top to bottom without falling. The next day I joined the beginners' class to learn the snowplough and the stem turn. My many falls left me black and blue with cuts on arms, elbows and face – not a pretty sight!

On the second or third day the party went to a tea dance at a large fashionable hotel, the Tambererhof, in our ski boots. This happened between five and seven each afternoon and was a great meeting place. It was there that I spied an incredibly attractive dark-haired beauty. I have always liked black hair, probably because I am fair myself!

With some arrogance I sent one of the party, Andrew Somerville, to ask her and her companion to join us. He reported back that her name was Edmée and she spoke only German and French. Using my rather basic French, I managed to persuade them to join our party for dinner that evening. At the time I asked her to choose which members of our party she would like to have dinner with. That decided, covered as I was with cuts and bruises I certainly didn't look very good and was very flattered that she seemed to enjoy my company and we had a number of evenings out together. The holiday was soon over, and we never got beyond the kissing stage. She returned to her job in Vienna and I to mine in London.

Later that year I asked Edmée to come and stay in a villa I had rented for several weeks in Santa Eulalia in Ibiza, which I had invited a number of friends to share. Among those who came was James Tulloch, who had separately invited two girls to join him, thinking only one would accept. He was rather surprised to find that they both decided to come!

To my delight Edmée decided to join the party as well. Very properly I had put her into a room of her own. After we had all gone to bed I heard shrieks from her room and found one of my friends climbing through the window. Not the action of a good guest!

One of the girls James had brought down was Angela Doody, an exceptionally pretty blonde with a flat in Lowndes Street. She subsequently lived in Monte Carlo with Christopher Stevenson, an international property agent, whom she later married. Soon after they were married they were both found shot dead in Monte Carlo in an apparent suicide pact. Stevenson had been doing business with some Russians and owed money to them, so there was some question as to whether it actually was suicide.

The holiday in Ibiza was a great success and having spent less than three weeks together I finished up asking Edmée to marry me. What we do when we are in love!

Before meeting Edmée I had been going out with Nicola Hemingway for some years. Nicola worked on the fashion page of the *Daily Telegraph*. She was an extraordinarily nice and very intelligent girl. Perhaps that's why she did not want to marry me!

Later, when Edmée came over to visit me in England, she took one look at the cottage and the flat in Kensington Church Street and suggested, quite rightly, that neither was appropriate as a family home.

Edmée and I went through a civil marriage on the 24th December 1968, followed by a weekend skiing just south of Vienna and in March 1969 a lavish three-day marriage ceremony at the Deutsche Ordanskirk in Vienna. The reception was at the Palais Pallavicini, a very elegant and beautiful palace in the heart of Vienna. I had driven there with my best man, David Wingfield, and my parents and a few close friends had flown out to join us. As most of my friends were not able to come to the wedding I decided I would have a reception in London so that they could all meet Edmée.

Before the wedding Edmée's father, an elegant and charming individual, had organised an evening drinking new wine in one of the wine cellars to the north of the city. It was called a Heuring. We had a great evening, which left us all heavily hung over for the wedding the next day. After the ceremony we departed on honeymoon skiing in Zurs, followed by a week in Gstaad.

For the reception in London I chose a large house, No. 6 Belgrave Square, where I was able to organise the champagne and catering facilities directly at a relatively competitive cost. The party was a great success, with lots of pretty girls and several exotics, including Janet, Countess of Cowley, although the cost put a severe strain on my financial resources.

A day or so before the party a very old friend of mine, Susie Orde, who was then looking after PR for the Savoy Hotel, telephoned me to ask if she could bring a VIP guest with her to the party. I told her it was a delayed wedding reception, but was happy for her to bring the VIP if she really wanted to. It turned out to be Christiaan Barnard, the South African surgeon who pioneered heart transplant surgery.

The party was in full swing when Christiaan came over to ask me if I would introduce him to a very beautiful blonde he had spotted at the other end of the room. It turned out to be an old friend called Caroline Monroe. I promised to do so when I had finished greeting some new arrivals. Five minutes later Caroline rushed up to me to ask if that really was Christiaan Barnard, and could she possibly be introduced to him – the first time that had ever happened to me. I performed the introduction. It was love at first sight and they were inseparable for three days, and probably three nights! In 1975 Caroline, whose ambition matched her beauty, married David Jacobs, the TV presenter, but later that year she was tragically killed in a car crash in the south of Spain.

Up to that time I had been in no hurry to marry again, as a married friend of mine had had a most unfortunate experience. A very glamorous ex-girlfriend of one of his close friends contacted him to ask for advice, and he was happy to accept her invitation to lunch. She wanted to know why this chap had broken off the relationship. My friend didn't think he could help, but paid for lunch, only to receive a couple of days later an invitation to a 'small dinner party' at her flat in Chelsea.

He told me it was a *very* small dinner party. The table had been laid for two, with an open bottle of champagne and smoked salmon, followed by fillet steak and some first-class claret – a seductive combination!

As they sat together after dinner enjoying coffee, the lady suggested they might be more comfortable upstairs. The seduction was complete! The happy beginning was followed by regular early weekday dinners, which continued for some six months. Risk and reward came together.

However, there were some uneasy moments when he got up to go home at 10 pm to find all the doors and windows locked and the keys hidden. This happened not once, but several times. Up till then he had not appreciated that this lovely creature had a history of instability, which rather frightened him.

Consequently, when he moved to Spain, he determined to end the relationship. However, left to his own devices in Marbella, he agreed to let her come down for a couple of weekends. The second of these brought disaster. She had read in the newspapers that he had inherited several million from an aunt. She decided that she was entitled to at least 1% of this and would tell his wife about the affair if he did not agree to pay her. She refused to leave Marbella until she had been remunerated.

After arguing the whole weekend, during which he maintained

that money had never been part of their relationship, he gave her a post-dated cheque and told her that if she cashed it she would never see him again. The outcome was not surprising. She cashed the cheque and he returned to the family home in Norfolk. On finding out when he was due back in England, she deluged the house with telephone calls insisting she would tell his wife unless he gave her more money. He informed her that he had already told his wife about the relationship (not true), and dared her to do her worst.

After a further series of calls, his wife naturally wanted to know what was happening. He told her that he had been blackmailed and that the relationship had been over for two months. Not surprisingly his wife was extremely upset, saying she wanted a divorce. He tried to dissuade her, to no avail. Unfortunately this led to the end of both the affair and the marriage. A cautionary tale.

1969 and 1970 were critical years from both a family and work perspective. Married life with Edmée had started off in the flat I used to share with David Wingfield in Kensington Church Street. This quickly proved not to be fit for purpose, and weekends were spent in Skirmett. Accordingly we decided to put the Skirmett cottage on the market and find something more appropriate in London.

We soon found a buyer for the cottage, selling it for over £9000, which gave us some £5000 to spend on a new property. After a long search we found a charming flat-fronted Georgian terraced house in Addison Avenue, Holland Park, for just over £17,000, taking out a mortgage of £12,000, much to the consternation of my parents, who worried that we were taking on too much debt. It suited us very well at the time as it was close enough to Holland Park to take children for walks and we had the key to Norland Square, where we were able to use the tennis court. We had just moved in when Alexis, our son, was born in March 1970, to be followed by Markus in April 1972.

Although the house was well situated, it was tall and thin, so was not ideal for a family, having too many stairs. It had a dining room and kitchen on the ground floor and bathroom and a sitting room on the first floor, with two bedrooms on the second floor. This was a lot of stairs for two young children, so we converted the basement to provide a playroom and extra bathroom. Unfortunately it did not have a garden, so some years later we bought the adjoining mews house with a garden immediately behind ours, incorporating the garden into our house and selling off the mews without a garden.

We lived there until 1981, when the property was sold to Amshel Rothschild and his new wife for £120,000. Sadly for them, the day after they took possession there was a massive storm which caused a flash flood in the basement. Although we had had a few problems with the drainage, we had not experienced anything quite so serious during the twelve years we had owned the property.

With Prince Michael of Kent and Edmée at Richard Wilkinson's wedding

CHAPTER 9

LONDON WEEKEND
1969-71

Early in 1969 an advertisement appeared in the *Financial Times* which would change the course of my life. It was for the post of Finance Director Designate at London Weekend Television. I applied and was interviewed by the joint managing directors, Michael Peacock, and Dr Tom Margerison, who had led a consortium that had won the commercial television franchise at the weekend in London.

The company had been in business just over a year, and up to that time finance and administration had been the responsibility of the company secretary, Cyril Orr. LWT already had a competent chief accountant, John Donovan, and an established accounting operation. The composition of the board was extremely heavyweight and included representatives of most of the major investors under the chairmanship of Aidan Crawley. It included two merchant bankers, David Montagu and Evelyn de Rothschild, and two Peers of the Realm, with a deputy chairman, Lord Campbell of Escan, Lord Hartwell, proprietor of the Daily Telegraph, David Astor, Owner of The Observer and Arnold Weinstock.

At the first interview in early 1969 I took a calculated risk by criticising the presentation of board papers considered at the last board meeting. When asked why I was leaving Modern Telephones, I had to be honest and tell them it was my lack of satisfaction with their accounting policies.

The final interview took place some weeks later, by which time they had sounded out Arnold Weinstock. Having taken action against GEC to ensure payment of a promised bonus some years earlier, I was a little apprehensive, but it appeared that he shared my views of Modern Telephones. This probably acted considerably to my advantage, as I was delighted to be offered the job, which I started in the spring of 1969.

It was an exciting time to be going into commercial television, particularly to be joining what appeared to be a highly competent creative team which had just been awarded the weekend ITV franchise for London.

Robert Fraser, Chairman of the ITA, conceived ITV as a public service broadcasting system, funded by a monopoly of advertising revenue with contracts awarded in accordance with the quality of programme performance and promise. The overall system, however, was extremely bureaucratic, with five major companies (two in London) and nine regional companies. Most of the programme output came from the five major companies, with production centres in major city centres. The nine regional companies had an obligation only to produce local news and current affairs. As a result there were fifteen separate companies, each with its own board of directors, programme controllers, finance, sales, administration and technical and engineering teams.

All fifteen contractors were responsible for local news and current affairs, with the major companies producing most of the peak programme output. In the case of the two London majors, Thames and LWT, each was responsible for approximately 43% of network programmes transmitted in their respective air time. This was equivalent to the London share of advertising revenue of the majors, with the balance coming from the other three majors during the weekday and weekend respectively. The regional companies paid the major companies in accordance with an hourly rate which was directly related to their respective advertising revenue.

In addition to its normal programme commitment, LWT hosted *World of Sport* on Saturday afternoons and shared the cost of ITN's news service.

The contracts also required that each of the contractors had to pay a tax/levy on advertising revenue irrespective of profitability. During 1969 and 1970 the profitability of the ITV contractors was under a great deal of pressure, largely due to the increased cost of programme production in colour. When I joined LWT the company had already acquired a site and planning consent for new offices and studios on the South Bank and was in negotiation with contractors and possible finance partners.

In the interim the company operated from rented offices at Station House, Wembley, and the old studios of Associated Rediffusion nearby. My first two or three weeks with LWT were spent getting to understand the ITV system, meeting the various departmental heads and familiarising myself with the inter-company programme and production arrangements. The creative team, led by its programme controller, Cyril Bennett, included Humphrey Burton, Frank Muir, Clive Irving and Jimmy Hill. The joint managing directors were Michael Peacock and Dr Tom Margerison.

I was very lucky to have drama producer John Hawkesworth to

take me through some of the intricacies of programme making. At that time *Upstairs Downstairs* was one of the LWT's key contributions to the ITV schedule, and I spent two most fascinating days on the set.

Having spent two months getting my feet under the desk, I took off to Ibiza with Edmée for a three-week summer holiday. I had rented a large villa, one I had regularly taken in the past.

In those days telecommunications in Ibiza were extremely primitive and the villa did not have a telephone. After an extremely relaxed holiday I returned to the UK to find LWT in turmoil and to discover that Michael Peacock, Cyril Bennett and most of the creative heads had resigned. They had left in protest at the board's wish that the company should be operated more commercially. Luckily I had not been contactable, so our holiday had not been ruined.

In September 1969, after several days of uncertainty, Tom Margerison was appointed Managing Director and Stella Richman was made Programme Controller in place of Cyril. Vic Gardiner was given greater responsibility as general manager. Brian Pover, the Chief Engineer, was given increased responsibility for building and equipping the new studios.

LWT had won its franchise on the strength of its programme promises, so with the resignation of so many talented programme makers the company was extremely vulnerable to having its franchise revoked by the IBA. We also had a number of the shareholders who were becoming extremely disenchanted with their investment. In particular Arnold Weinstock had apparently attended some early board meetings and was not impressed by what he had seen and heard.

During the latter months of 1969 and the first nine months of 1970, LWT was run by an executive committee comprising Tom Margerison, Stella Richman, Guy Payne, Vic Gardiner, Brian Pover and myself, with Cyril Orr as Company Secretary. Construction of the new studios on the South Bank had begun and arrangements had been made to finance the building of the studios and offices with CIN (Coal Industry Nominees), the National Coal Board pension fund. Planning consent had been obtained for 110,000 square feet of offices, only half of which was required for the TV operation. As some 65% of the construction costs related to the studio complex, the rental value of the offices was critical to justify the capital expenditure on the whole project.

Unfortunately planning consent had been granted on the basis that all the office space was to be used exclusively by LWT, and it could not therefore be sublet to an outside party. Accordingly an appointment was made for David Montagu, Chairman of Samuel Montagu, and me to go and see the Minister of Environment, Nicholas Ridley, to try to persuade him to release us from the planning restriction, so that we could sublet the nine floors of surplus offices, which would allow us to complete the project. The interview took place in Whitehall, where we were shown into a cavernous office where Nicholas Ridley sat at the end of an enormous room behind an extremely large desk, attended by a couple of acolytes.

Although the company was at that time making a small profit on a month-by-month basis, the financial position of LWT was not strong and we desperately required this consent in order to persuade CIN to put up the extra finance required to complete the project. We were delighted to hear a few days later that the trip to

Whitehall had been successful and we were able to sublet the surplus space and conclude the financing arrangement with CIN.

In September 1970 Arnold Weinstock decided he had had enough, and sold his shareholding to Rupert Murdoch of News International. Murdoch immediately took over the chairmanship of the executive committee running the company and instituted a review of all the operations, bringing in Bert Hardy, a senior News International executive, to review the sales operations, previously the responsibility of Guy Payne. The production, engineering, finance and administrative administrations all passed with flying colours, but there were three areas in which the company was weak: programmes, sales, and control of the South Bank project, where I had been extremely critical of the adequacy of the various reports produced by Guy Payne. Luckily I had put my criticisms in writing, both to Payne and to Tom Margerison.

During this period regular executive meetings took place on a weekly basis. At one of these meetings Rupert Murdoch informed us that News International would be underwriting an equity rights issue of £500,000 in non-voting shares, to increase the share capital from £2 million to £2.5 million. He had apparently persuaded the other shareholders not to take up their rights and to allow News International to increase its equity shareholding to approximately 35% (although only 7.5% of this was in voting shares).

Having prepared a two-year forward cash flow projection, I argued that LWT did not need the extra capital. I had discussed this with my executive colleagues before the meetings, so I was disappointed that I was not supported by them as they had previously agreed to do. After the meeting Murdoch told me he was not prepared to be involved with the company and sort out its problems unless he had a worthwhile interest. I was amazed that the other shareholders had agreed to allow their shareholding to be diluted, but then Rupert Murdoch could be very persuasive!

In February 1971 Stella Richman produced a review of LWT's programme output. It was an extremely negative report, and soon afterwards she was asked to leave the company. Guy Payne was also given the boot along with his financial sidekick, and I was at last given responsibility for the finance side of the South Bank project, with Vic Gardiner and Brian Pover looking after the technical and engineering aspects.

Some two weeks later Tom Margerison was also asked to leave. During 1970 he had attended meetings with other major companies, and it had become apparent that LWT's interests and those of the other major contractors were not always identical with many of ITV's key ratings programmes being scheduled mid-week rather than at the weekend. This was not helped by Tom Margerison's habit of lecturing the other more experienced managing directors in a way which certainly didn't help LWT's own interests.

Early in 1971 John Freeman was appointed Chairman. He had apparently been persuaded by David Frost and David Montagu to take on the job. He had had an extremely distinguished career, having been editor of the *New Statesman*, a Cabinet Minister in the Attlee Labour Government and High Commissioner for India. He had also been a seriously high-profile interviewer and had just finished his two-year term as British Ambassador in Washington. We could not have asked for a better chairman to introduce stability and restore confidence in the fledgling company. However, we were short of a programme controller.

The management changes which had taken place, in particular

the acquisition by News International of the GEC stake and the rights issue, had caused a great deal of consternation at the IBA. Despite the reassurance provided by the appointment of John Freeman, LWT was asked to re-apply for its franchise.

The meeting took place on 22nd April 1971 at IBA's headquarters in Brompton Road. The members of the authority were seated on one side of a large horseshoe-shaped table with the LWT team on the other side. The LWT team, headed by John Freeman, included Rupert Murdoch, Lord Campbell, David Montagu, Evelyn de Rothschild, Vic Gardiner, Brian Pover, Cyril Orr and myself.

John Freeman made a faultless presentation, acknowledging that the company had underestimated some of the difficulties and its own shortcomings, but claiming some success in comedy, drama, sports and arts programmes and a degree of technical achievement. We all breathed a sigh of relief when we heard later that the franchise had not been revoked.

The arrival of John Freeman and the return of Cyril Bennett as programme controller at the beginning of 1971 provided a cornerstone for LWT's future success. We had in place a first-class team on the programme side. There was Cyril, ably assisted by John Blyton, programme management, and Eric Flackfield and Warren Breach, programme presentation and planning, all of whom had had a lot of television experience. The general manager was Vic Gardiner and Roger Appleton was Chief Engineer, while Peter Cazalet was production controller. Cyril Orr was the company secretary, and I at last had full control of the financial direction of all the operations of the company, including responsibilities for all subsidiary activities.

With the move into colour I could see a bright future for commercial TV, despite the constraints under which it had to operate. We had a monopoly of television advertising revenue, with the mandated limit of seven minutes per hour, and with colourisation the potential of ever-expanding demand with a limited supply.

Bert Hardy from News International had brought Ron Miller into the company as new sales manager – young and very talented – to replace the charming but laid-back Guy Payne. Ron had previously worked for Anglia TV and had the right East London barrow-boy approach to selling airtime, which worked well to maximise advertising revenue for LWT.

LWT's programmes were beginning to have an impact on the weekend schedules, with success in drama with *Manhunt*, *Upstairs Downstairs* and *Budgie* and in comedy with *The Fenn Street Gang*, *Please Sir* and the *Doctor* series. *World of Sport*, under the able guidance of Jimmy Hill and John Bromley, were attracting good weekend ratings. We were only short of audience-winning programmes from the other three major companies transmitting at the weekend.

In addition to our heavyweights there was a number of small shareholders, including *The Spectator*, which had several years earlier been bought by an old friend of mine, Harry Creighton. Harry had made his money in the machine tool industry and I had come across him a number of times in my Staveley days, when I was closing down Craven Brothers and Kendall & Gent.

The Spectator had frequent lunches at their offices, and after I joined LWT Harry had invited me several times, quizzing me about Staveley and ITV. After joining Modern Telephones I had been trying to orchestrate a takeover of Staveley Industries, which I considered had squandered large amounts of capital in trying to support the UK machine tool industry rather than concentrating on its profitable activities of chemicals, electrical contracting and foundries. This had resulted in a partial bid by Oliver Jessell and some extra income, but it produced a fraction of which I might have made had there been a complete takeover.

In January 1971, during one of the *Spectator* lunches, Harry asked me what he should do with his LWT shareholding. Rupert Murdoch had given shares to both John Freeman and Vic Gardiner. I told Harry he should not sell and that I was full of confidence in the company, but if he decided to do so, I would be a potential buyer.

Two weeks later I had a telephone call from my own stockbroker, Duncan Barber to say "I got some shares in LWT – are you interested?"

"It depends on how many and at what price" I answered.

"It's 25,000 shares and the price is £2.09" he replied.

I told him that the highest price to date had been £2, although Rupert Murdoch had in 1970 underwritten a rights issue at £1 a share.

"That's the price if you want them" he said. "I'll give you till tomorrow at 12 noon to make up your mind, otherwise I will offer them elsewhere."

What was I to do? I desperately wanted to acquire shares in LWT. Rupert Murdoch had not offered me any – I don't think he rated ex-public school product very highly! I had a £12,000 mortgage and a new son and I had just made a little money in dealing in copper, the only commodity transaction I ever did. However, this transaction required a payment of £40,000 to £50,000 within two weeks.

I thought hard. My brother John had just sold some property and I knew he was temporarily in funds. I telephoned him to tell him of the project and, after some persuasion, he agreed to come in with me on a 50-50 basis and buy 20,000 of the shares. I then telephoned Johnny Jones, an old friend who worked for Ionian Bank, a small merchant bank, who agreed that the bank would put up the other 50%. I then telephoned the broker, agreeing to buy 20,000 shares. I told John, who had last-minute reservations, that we were legally committed and assured him I would underwrite any potential loss he might sustain when the transaction was completed.

His reactions were understandable. The rights issue at one pound per share had only taken place some six months earlier, and he was wholly reliant on my knowledge of the company. However he arranged for his lawyer to produce a formal legal agreement, in which I pledged the equity in my house in Addison Avenue as security. We had bought 20,000 shares at £2.09 for just over £40,000, and although that does not seem so much today, in 1971 it was enough to buy two four-bedroom houses in Kensington, which today would cost at least £4 million each.

A couple of months later in September 1971, just as we were going on holiday, John told me that despite our legal agreement and my assurances he wanted me to sell his shares. Despite my protestations, pointing out it would place me in an invidious position and telling him he was missing the opportunity of a lifetime, I was unable to persuade him to hold on.

Consequently, and with a great deal of reluctance, I asked Michael Richardson of Cazenove to sell John's half share at £3 per share. After a couple of weeks Michael telephoned me to say he had had no takers. I asked him if he had talked to all the existing shareholders, or offered them to Rupert Murdoch. He subsequently did so and reported that Rupert Murdoch was not interested. I was in trouble.

My brother John was leaning heavily on me to make a sale, as he needed the capital for another project. What was I to do? With considerable trepidation, I telephoned Michael Richardson to suggest he should have a further chat with Rupert Murdoch, pointing out to him that a payment of £3 per share would establish a new price level for the shares and make his existing investment in LWT worth more than £1 million more than he had paid. The logic was persuasive, and Michael subsequently telephoned me to say that Murdoch had bought the 10,000 shares at £30,000. This allowed me to repay John's investment together with half the profit. But at what cost to me?

At the next board meeting, when the share transfer for the original purchase of the 20,000 shares at £2.09 came before the board for approval, the shit really hit the fan. Rupert Murdoch, having paid £3 per share a month earlier, was incandescent with rage. Apparently, unknown to me, the other major shareholders had agreed privately that Murdoch should be allowed to buy any LWT shares which became available. Who was the Ionian Bank, who had pulled a fast one on him? I kept my head down. He was bound to find out. Only he and I knew that he had paid £3 per share several weeks later.

Immediately after the board meetings I went to see John Freeman. Despite my detailed explanations, he was not at all impressed, to put it mildly. He told me I would have to apologise in person to Rupert Murdoch.

With some trepidation I made an appointment to see Murdoch

in his Fleet Street office. I explained the situation to him and told him I'd been badly let down by my brother as it had been my intention to be a long-term holder of the shares. I went on to say I did not believe I had anything to apologise to him for, but I apologised anyway. I also told him of my disappointment at not being allocated shares by him when he had done this for John Freeman, and of my considerable confidence in the company's future.

I also pointed out to him that he had established a new value for the shares at £3, which was not wholly disadvantageous to the value of his shareholding in the company. Despite a frosty reception, we finished up talking about the issues on which we had disagreed at executive meetings in the six months to March 1971. He had attended most of these meetings, at which a few of my colleagues would disagree with his views. I seemed to be the odd one out. I believed he probably respected a direct reply to a direct question.

That incident in the summer of 1971 might not have been helpful to my otherwise excellent relations with John Freeman, who had then been with LWT some nine months, as it put my integrity in question.

John Freeman was a first-class chairman, highly intelligent, very well organised and an extremely good delegator. He did not, however, like surprises. He would use our pre-board meetings to iron out any differences of opinion between the executive members prior to the full board meetings, at which most non-executive directors were normally present.

At that time, although both I and the sales manager, Ron Miller, were key members of the executive board, we were not formally board members, although we attended all board meetings as a matter of course. So when some months later John Freeman told me that it was likely that Ron was to be formally appointed to the board, but not me, I was not amused. He mentioned that two non-executive directors were likely to oppose the appointment. One of them was Lord Campbell, with whom I'd never really got on, and the other was Rupert Murdoch, for obvious reasons.

Discussing the issue with Cyril Bennett, who had by then become an extremely good friend, he suggested to me that although he personally did not rate board membership very highly, the best thing would be for me to go and see Rupert Murdoch and have it out with him if I thought it so important. Accordingly I made an appointment to see Murdoch, who commented that he did not understand why John Freeman should think he would not support my appointment. I told him that if I were to do my job properly I needed the authority to do so, and reminded him of our achievements since joining the company in 1969.

In the event, after some anxious moments, I had Murdoch's support. With Ron Miller I was appointed to the board a few days later.

Fortunately my relationship with John improved significantly after that. On one occasion when we were entertaining London Conservative MPs, he turned to me and said "It is our opportunity to demonstrate to the Government a significant Anglo Saxon presence within ITV." On another occasion in the late seventies, when we were entertaining our non-executive directors and their wives, he produced a short biography of each one. I remember very clearly his description of Lord Hartwell's wife, which read "Pamela Hartwell, majestic, faded beauty: a significant force behind the throne." I learnt so much working with John. He always appeared to be a relaxed and spontaneous speaker, speaking without notes.

He had remarkable recall. Before a major speech he would lock himself in his office to prepare and rehearse the speech, then give a remarkable performance which appeared to be totally "off the cuff".

Cyril Bennett was a great character – flamboyant, clever, articulate and sometimes very funny. At that time it was normal practice for each of the directors to circulate to other executive board members copies of the letters which they had sent during the previous week in a weekly file. His copy letter file was always a source of great entertainment, and was always eagerly awaited each week. He was an amazingly competent controller of programmes, with a natural ability and remarkable creativity.

He was also a great raconteur. One of his best stories concerned Harold Macmillan's visit to the Rediffusion studios. The Prime Minister was being taken around the studios by the MD, an ex-naval man, Captain Brownlow, who never listened to anything anybody said. Harold Macmillan ended up having to be provided with a dry pair of trousers because of Captain Brownlow's inability to hear the PM's wish to go to the loo!

I had managed to get Cyril out of a major financial commitment on one occasion, which had helped to cement our relationship. For someone so capable of managing a multi-million programme budget, his own financial affairs seemed to take a very low priority in his life. He was the only programme controller I tried to persuade to spend more money on programmes rather than less.

CHAPTER 10

TRIUMPH AND TRAGEDY
AT LONDON WEEKEND
1971-77

1971 and 1972 involved a lot of activity for us all at LWT. Our main concern was the completion of the new offices and studios on the South Bank, which were formally opened by the Duke of Kent in the summer. At that time they were the most modern, up-to-date and best equipped studio and office complex in the UK. John Freeman, Vic Gardiner, Cyril Orr, the company secretary, and I moved to the 13th floor of the newly named Kent House, now renamed The London Television Centre and ITV Headquarters.

My office was between those of Vic Gardiner and John Freeman. Gardiner had the corner office facing north and east, where we shared secretaries and an outside office.

LWT's programmes became increasingly successful, both in ratings and critical appreciation. Our current affairs programme, *Weekend World*, was presented by Peter Jay and became a regular feature at midday on Sundays.

In 1973 we were all systems go. I had been lucky enough to recruit Paul Gibson, a first-class computer manager with O&M experience, during a period of rapid computer innovation and at a time when the concept of central all-singing all-dancing computer systems appeared to be both costly and inappropriate to the operation of a commercial television franchise. This was because the costs of programmes and overheads were not directly related to the revenue that could be earned from advertising. Furthermore, the highest programme costs were those of local programmes without contribution from our network colleagues, as were current affairs and arts programmes with limited audience appeal; these were however integral to our franchise obligations and contract renewal.

Accordingly, we designed our computer systems as separate entities to service the specific needs of the company's various operations. This was particularly important for the sales operation, where airtime was being sold up to 5.30 pm on Friday and it was essential that sales management had a minute-by-minute record of what had been sold and what remained to be sold before the weekend. This enabled sales management to devise the appropriate premiums/discount arrangements to maximise airtime sales income.

In 1973, despite the increase in advertising revenue, ITV still had to contend with an exchequer levy based on turnover. Although this had been reduced in 1971, it still remained at a high level. Pressure was therefore being brought to bear on the IBA and Government for a change in the levy from one based on turnover to one based on profits.

During 1973 Brian Walden, who had taken over from Peter Jay as presenter of *Weekend World*, was extremely helpful in arranging for me to meet Geoffrey Howe, the Chancellor of the Exchequer, after he had been interviewed on the programme. This enabled me to discuss with him the merits of a profits-based levy. In the event a change in the levy to one based on profits rather than turnover was enacted in the 1974 Broadcasting Act. I would like to think that my talk to the Chancellor might have contributed to this change.

Although 66.7% of profits in excess of 2% of advertising revenue, coupled with corporation tax of 40%, resulted in marginal tax on ITV's company profits of 84%, this was a great deal better than one based on turnover. This was the rate that lasted until 1986, by which time the ITV contractors had paid a levy of some £500 million to the Government. The change in levy did however present a serious opportunity to make programmes which had international sales appeal, as profits from overseas sales were free of the Exchequer levy.

In 1969 Richard Price Television Associates had been appointed by LWT to sell our programmes overseas, and together we set about addressing ways in which this might be improved and enhanced. Although our programmes produced in 1973 and 1974 had achieved critical acclaim, it was only the situation comedy output which was selling well abroad. Accordingly I tried to persuade Cyril Bennett that we should be spending a lot more on action adventure series with significant overseas sales appeal. This we found was not easy, as the principal overseas sales market was the USA, where at least 69 episodes had to be produced to make a pre-sale to an American network possible. Such shows as *Upstairs Downstairs* did not achieve a US network sale and the only US sale possible was to PBS, the public broadcasting service, barely covering the residual costs involved.

Nevertheless, Cyril Bennett achieved his just recognition when LWT won seven BAFTA awards in March 1974 – unprecedented for an independent television contractor. In that year Stanley

Baxter, David Bell, Peter Barkworth, Humphrey Burton, Lydia Bateman and Peter Jay were all honoured. This was a massive achievement, which was never subsequently bettered by any ITV contractor. It was a wonderful testament to a remarkably gifted programme controller.

The BAFTA-winning LWT team 1974 – left to right,
David Bell, Bill McPherson, Stanley Baxter, Cyril Bennett, Lydia Bateman, Peter Barkworth,
Humphrey Burton, Peter Jay

Later that year Brian Tesler, who had achieved considerable success as Programme Controller of Thames TV, was appointed by John Freeman as managing director, John having previously carried out both functions as managing director and chairman. Michael Grade had joined LWT the previous year to run the light entertainment department at the age of thirty, having worked for the Daily Mirror as a journalist and as a theatrical agent with his father, Leslie Grade, before joining LWT. John Birt was then head of current affairs, where he had made *Weekend World* into a major event.

With a change in the levy we were all beginning to feel much more comfortable, and the company was beginning to achieve good profits and even better cash flow.

At that time the franchise awards were determined by a "beauty contest"; the company was judged more by the quality of its current affairs, arts and drama than by popular programmes with significant audience appeal. In the early 1970s LWT had gained ratings success with an annual output of some 100 half hours of situation comedy - *Please Sir, On the Buses, Doctor in the House, The Fenn Street Gang*, etc. We had also produced some outstanding dramas, notably *Upstairs Downstairs* and *A Married Man*, but we did not have much help from the other three majors transmitting at the weekend, whose more popular product was scheduled largely during the weekday in more protected slots.

This became a source of constant friction between LWT and our industry colleagues, particularly when we wanted a particular series to be commissioned for the weekend. It required a lot of diplomatic bargaining, both by MDs and at programme controller level.

In addition to producing some 43% of peak time network programmes at the weekend, LWT hosted *World of Sport*, which in the early years was run by Jimmy Hill and John Bromley and earned LWT valuable income from our industry colleagues. It was, however, the source of some friction with the other companies, who were always looking for ways of reducing the benefit enjoyed by LWT from its origination.

The appointment of Brian Tesler as Managing Director added considerable strength to LWT's management team through the addition of his wide experience in the industry and his talent and diplomatic skills. Although the company had operated extremely well under John Freeman's excellent combined role as chairman and chief executive, it was, I believe, important that Brian Tesler, with his programme expertise, experience and diplomatic skills, should take responsibility for the overall direction of our television franchise.

However, it is possible that Cyril Bennett perceived Brian's appointment as a vote of no confidence in him at LWT, as we had in effect appointed someone else to oversee the critical programme output of the company. We can never be sure whether this influenced what happened next.

In September 1976 a two-day conference of programme heads of department was organised. Although I was not present, I understand that Cyril had been heavily criticised during the conference and had taken a lot of flak. After the conference he returned to his third-floor apartment in Kingston to change for dinner. His driver, Vic Calder, was I believe due to pick him up at around eight o'clock. By the time he got there, Cyril had fallen from the window and was dead.

Cyril might well have been leaning out of the window to see whether his car had arrived when the accident occurred. He had been taking anti-depressants, which might well have affected his balance, making him trip and fall from the window.

It has been suggested that it was suicide. It is true that Cyril had family problems, that he had had a couple of very difficult days and that he suffered from depression, but I cannot believe that he had the physical courage to take his own life. The fact that he was due to take out one of his children the next day was for me the deciding factor. He was a fond parent and a devoted father and would never have let down his child.

Memory plays tricks, and the perspective of those closest to the event is often clouded by irrelevant factors. I hope I have recalled accurately the sequence of events which led up to Cyril Bennett's tragic death. Who can say what effect the above events might have had on the sensitive character of this talented but highly volatile individual?

Cyril Bennett always seemed to be in some form of predicament and always seemed short of cash. His death was a tragic loss for his family and for LWT as, for all his eccentricity, he was a lovely man, an excellent colleague and a very good friend.

In 1977 I was making preparations to float the company on the London Stock Exchange. With two eminent merchant bankers on the board in the persons of David Montagu and Evelyn de Rothschild, we were well equipped to join the main stock market. We had valuable help from the company broker, Cazenove & Co, with Samuel Montagu as our house merchant banker and the flotation was a modest success, with the shares moving to a small premium soon after the float.

In those days, with a monopoly of advertising revenue, the company's cash flow had grown progressively and we were making good profits despite the Exchequer levy. I was delighted to be given the task of finding suitable alternative investments, as in those days we were precluded by the IBA from acquiring another ITV contractor, a potential merger with Anglia Television having been vetoed by the IBA. The acquisition objective was to find investments which would complement that of an independent television franchise and where an annual profit stream could be created which was not dependent on advertising revenue.

A large number of possible acquisitions were considered and rejected. There was one, however, which I found most interesting: a greetings card company called W N Sharp. It appeared to me to be an amazing bargain, with substantial cash balances, an asset value in excess of the share price and a divided yield of about 10% per annum.

We made an approach through Samuel Montagu at a 30% premium, and were immediately rejected. Unfortunately I was unable to persuade either myself or John Freeman or the others to go to the 100 per cent premium requested, and sadly we did not proceed with the acquisition. W N Sharp was subsequently sold for a higher price, but a large part of it was covered by cash resources and the sale of the boardroom pictures. It was a great missed opportunity.

Another acquisition possibility was introduced by Jeremy Potter, at the time chief executive of ITP. This was the travel company Page and Moy, whose founders Leon Page and Tony Moy were keen to sell. They had built up the company, a large part of whose holidays were marketed through direct sales in the TV Times. I was keen that they should remain shareholders, and during the negotiation I agreed that LWT should buy 60% of their shareholding, with the obligation that they should retain the balance for at least five years with options to acquire the remaining 40% shareholding on a multiple of future profits. This proved to be a first-class investment, yielding good dividends. Our investment was subsequently sold to Barclaycard some ten years later in 1988 at a good profit.

Soon after we had purchased the shareholding in Page and Moy, my brother John's father-in-law brought to my attention the possibility of purchasing the publisher Hutchinson Ltd. Hutchinson was a large general publisher with an output of some 600 titles a year, including books by Frederick Forsyth and Len Deighton, a sporting imprint and an educational and maps division. The company also had extensive printing and distribution operations in Tiptree in Essex.

The profit record of the company was mixed, although when we acquired it the profit shown in the previous year amounted to some £600,000 and the acquisition price was below the book net asset value. After the acquisition an evaluation revealed that many of the books held in stock were in excess of the likely demand, and substantial write-off of stock values became necessary. Profitability was patchy; while a number of prestige authors were producing good profits, most of them were absorbed by those who didn't.

In-house printing and distribution also appeared to be more expensive than could be achieved elsewhere. Although maps, sporting titles and educational publishing consistently produced a profit, this was at a relatively low level.

At the time of acquisition, Hutchinson's chairman was a solicitor called Bimbi Holt, whose doubtful claim to fame was to be in the Guinness Book of Records as the biggest beneficiary under a will of an unrelated person. I'm sure that the fact that he was also her legal adviser had nothing to do with the bequest!

Hutchinson was at that time a large and fragmented operation, and I suspect that in order to maximise production through their printing, publicity and marketing operations they needed to produce a significant volume of books each year. They also needed to support young and unproven authors to replace those whose popularity was waning. Unfortunately too many of their authors' books did not make money, and the cost of producing them in house was a great deal higher than printing them in the Far East.

How was the problem of low profitability to be resolved? In addition to surplus stocks in the UK, the marketing operations in Australia proved to have had more books shipped from the UK, which had to be written off. The solution was to find another publisher with more talented editorial directors and without the commitment to printing and distribution operations.

Some years later, after a lot of research, we were lucky enough to find just such a company in the form of Century Publishing, under the direction of Anthony Cheetham. Accordingly the decision was taken to merge the two operations to form one smaller and more profitable operation, with many of Hutchinson's existing facilities being closed. Seven years afterwards the merged company was sold to Random House and most of our investment was recovered.

CHAPTER 11

CHANGES AT THE TOP AT
LONDON WEEKEND

1977-93

1977 was the year Michael Grade became LWT's Programme Controller, at the age of 33. Articulate, highly intelligent and full of confidence, Grade possessed an enviable talent for selecting programmes and scheduling them to achieve the highest audience potential within the weekend schedule.

In this he was ably assisted by Eric Flackfield and John Blyton, with John Birt running the Current Affairs Department. At that time *Weekend World*, presented by the multi-talented Brian Walden, was a vital and important element of LWT's public service commitment.

The youthful Grade was not however an unqualified success. Production budgets were constantly being exceeded and a number of potential situation comedy series were discontinued after a limited number of episodes without being given time to become established. Additionally one or two expensive variety programmes had to be written off, and the cost of football at the weekend was significantly increased by the agreement of a new contract with the Football League without the authority of the board or of the other major contractors.

Accordingly, despite an 18% increase in advertising revenue in 1978/79, profit did not increase, and the LWT non-executive directors became extremely critical of programme performance. The additional programme expenditure had not resulted in the expected improvement in quality or generated increased audiences. At the same time LWT's current affairs department was involved in Scottish contempt litigation with an official secrets débâcle, which further undermined LWT's management's reputation for competence.

This led to John Freeman writing to all executive colleagues on 20th July 1979 outlining his concerns, followed by a series of meetings of the executive board to agree what could be done to rectify the situation. This in turn led to a tightening of our procedures and the private briefing of a number of the key non-executive directors.

In 1981 Michael Grade left LWT to join Embassy TV in Los Angeles, where he was paid considerably more than the disappointingly low salaries paid by LWT to executive directors and management at that time.

In 1982 Michael was succeeded as Programme Controller by John Birt, a very different character. Unlike Michael Grade's show business background, Birt had come up through current affairs. He had been educated by the Jesuits at St Mary's College Liverpool and St Catherine's College Oxford. He had joined LWT in 1972 from Granada, having edited *World in Action* and produced *The Frost Programme*. At LWT he had run the current affairs department, where he had achieved considerable success with *Weekend World*, a vital component of LWT's current affairs output.

In those days current affairs programmes and local programmes were an important element of LWT's public service commitment, by which the company's franchise renewal prospects were judged by the IBA. Unfortunately, however, they were programmes which generated little advertising revenue. It was therefore very much a matter of subjective judgement how much of the company's resources should be used to produce peak-time programmes which generated advertising revenue, overseas sales and network income and how much should be devoted to current affairs programmes.

Not surprisingly, the allocation of programme-making funds was regarded by John Birt as his sole responsibility, which gave rise to considerable friction between us. His schedule was organised in such a way that he never seemed to be available when I wanted him to spend time going through his programme plans with me. There were a number of occasions when I wanted him to include programme series with considerable overseas sales potential in the weekend schedule. This was achieved only after intervention by John Freeman. I had become particularly concerned about the substantial sums we were spending on current affairs and local programmes using resources which, in my opinion, might be better employed in producing entertainment and situation comedy.

In an attempt to resolve the situation, John Freeman arranged a weekend away with Brian Tesler, John Birt and myself so that we could discuss the most appropriate allocation of the company's resources, both to maximise advertising revenue and to ensure renewal of LWT franchise. This happened in 1982 at Grave Tree Manor. I remember very little about the weekend other than a comment by John Birt that I was extremely lucky to have been born with a silver spoon in my mouth! My reply was that the spoon was silver-plated and there were five mouths trying to share it at the same time, so he should not consider me to be particularly privileged.

I also remember suggesting to him that because of his great talent for news, factual and current affairs programmes, he would be much better running the BBC's current affairs than a commercial TV franchise. Apparently up to that time he had not considered this to be a possibility. However it proved to be a prophetic statement, as in 1987 he left LWT to be appointed Deputy Director General of the BBC. In my view it was the perfect appointment for somebody of his talent, and one for which I believe he was uniquely suited.

In 1983 John Freeman had announced that he would be retiring the following year. Up to that time it had been expected that he would be succeeded by Roger Harrison, MD of Observer Newspapers, for whom I had a great liking and respect. In the event John announced that he would be proposing as his successor Sir Christopher Bland, an ex-deputy chairman of IBA, who had joined the LWT board some two years earlier. I had a great deal of respect for Christopher's strong character and commercial ability, having had him to shoot and fish on a couple of occasions, and I was aware that he was an extremely ambitious and charming, yet driven, character. In expressing my preference for Roger Harrison I probably did myself no favours. In the event Christopher was appointed to succeed John as chairman in 1984.

Christopher Bland's appointment marked a sea change in the company's operations. Whereas John Freeman had been happy to delegate, Christopher, not surprisingly, wanted to be much more involved with the city and with our major subsidiaries and shareholders. Up to that time this had been one of my responsibilities.

Our relations with the city had been guided by David Montagu at Samuel Montagu and Stephen Carden at Cazanove, two highly respected individuals with whom I had a first-class relationship. Despite Christopher's initial re-examination of these appointments, I am glad to say that Montagus and Cazanoves continued as our primary advisors.

What was even more positive was the merger of Hutchinson, bought several years earlier, with Century Publishing. The ownership of Hutchinson had not been wholly satisfactory: I was therefore more than happy to see Hutchinson merge with Century Publishing under the control of Anthony Cheetham, with a subsequent sale, some years later, to Random House.

LWT's involvement in Hutchinson had not been very profitable. Although the maps, sports and educational publishing sides made money, they contributed only a small part of Hutchinson's turnover, with printing and distribution depending on the success of major authors such as Frederick Forsyth, Len Deighton and James West. There was also a problem in Australia from the overstocking of titles.

Within ITV the need for the 15 ITV contractors to act together required an elaborate series of committees to agree contentious inter-company and industry issues. This was also achieved through shareholder representation on the boards of ITP (Independent Television Publications) and ITN, the ITV network news channel. In the case of ITP effective management was by a chairman's committee, of which I was the major companies' representative, and which oversaw the sale of TV Times in the late 80s.

A special committee was also put in place to organise, with Stanhope Properties, the appropriate financial structure for the development of the new ITN studios in Grays Inn Road. One of the advantages of this site was the large amount of space below ground, ideal for sound-proofed studios. However, with a large part of the capital cost of the development attributable to the studio complex rather than the offices, for which an open market value was almost impossible to establish, financing presented a challenge.

My solution, as chairman of that committee, was to link the financing almost exclusively to the rental value of the office blocks above ground, on a similar basis to that used for the financing of the LWT Studios on the South Bank. Consequently, when the Queen and Prince Philip opened the the studios in 1990, I was part of the reception committee and was able to meet and talk to both of them. Unfortunately my video of the event was damaged in a flood in my house in Hannington Wick in 2007, together with a video of white water rafting on the Zambezi in 1994.

In 1969, when LWT had won its franchises, a subsidiary, LWT 1, had been formed to expand overseas sales potential of its planned programme output under the direction of Stella Richman. At that time it became very quickly apparent that the scale of the operation was wholly disproportionate to the overseas sales potential of LWT's programmes, in particular its drama and entertainment. Richard Price Television Associates was our overseas sales agent.

Back in 1969 the general manager, Vic Gardener, and I had joined the board of LWT 1's considerably reduced operation, which was responsible for monitoring and guiding the sale of LWT's product overseas. This gave me a more detailed insight into the marketing of product overseas, and in later years the value of pre-sales, which required the close involvement of LWT's programme makers. This became increasingly important as the cost of drama production escalated above a level which could be justified from the transmissions in the UK.

With the appointment of Christopher Bland, RPTA were relieved of this responsibility and a controlling interest in a Los

Angeles-based American sales operation, Silverbach-Lazarus, a small distribution company, was acquired. Given the sound relationship I had established with Richard Price of RPTA, I was disappointed with the decision to replace them. Despite their extensive Hollywood connections, it was doubtful whether Silverbach-Lazarus could be of much help to us. However it was a sporting opportunity, and subsequently I was lucky enough to persuade Messrs Silverbach-Lazarus to buy back for £1 the 60% shareholding we had acquired. I was happy to be relieved of LWT's guarantee of their substantial overdraft.

With the exception of the acquisition of Silverbach-Lazarus, I found my views totally in line with those of Christopher

PM in his office at LWT

concerning our subsidiary activities and came to respect his consummate commercial ability. He proved to be a highly effective chairman. This applied particularly in the run-up to the franchise renewals in 1989, when some very brave decisions had to be taken concerning the future structure of the company.

Page & Moy was LWT's first acquisition and had been profitable throughout, Leon Page having joined the LWT board. However the capital reorganisation necessitated the disposal of all LWT's non-core franchising assets, including Page & Moy, giving LWT a useful profit.

The departure of John Birt to the BBC in 1987 involved Brian Tesler temporarily taking over as Programme Director until Greg Dyke, who had previously worked in the current affairs department, was appointed Programme Controller. Greg had made his name rescuing TV AM in 1983/84 with the help of Roland Rat and had been Programme Director at Southern TV for the previous two years. He was extremely talented, both creatively and commercially, with remarkable communication skills and considerable scheduling talent. He took a very commercial approach to programme making, a welcome change after the formality and inflexibility of his predecessor.

John Birt, despite his considerable intellect and talent for current affairs, had not been an easy character to work with, rarely changing his mind. I therefore could not have been more delighted when Greg Dyke was appointed to take his place.

I actually believe John Birt was partly responsible for Margaret Thatcher's decision to put the ITV commercial franchises up for auction. When LWT had to cover an interview at Downing Street, the current affairs department sent two teams of cameramen, sound, etc to cover this half-hour interview. For a similar length interview, NBC from the United States sent only four people. This must have convinced Mrs Thatcher that ITV was profligate with its resources and needed complete reorganisation. Her decision to auction the franchises previously allocated on the basis of past and present fulfilment of public services commitments presented a lethal challenge to the 15 ITV contractors. It did however present LWT with a major opportunity.

At that time there were only four TV channels, BBC 1, BBC 2, ITV and Channel 4, two of which were funded by the licence fee. ITV and Channel 4 were funded by advertising revenue, with extensive obligations to transmit high-quality educational, drama, arts and documentaries and local programmes. Effectively both BBC and ITV were to a greater or lesser extent run as public service broadcasters.

The auction process provided major difficulties for the existing franchise companies, which had been set up primarily to fulfil their public service obligations but not as wholly commercial broadcasters. New applicants without this production and overhead commitment were in a better position to outbid the existing franchise holders.

Had the bidding process developed on a strictly cash basis, it is unlikely that any of the existing franchise holders would have retained their franchises. Fortunately, however, the IBA managed to persuade the Government that programme quality, expert management and financial competence should also be major factors in the award of the franchises. This helped to balance the competition from the new bidders.

In preparation for the contract competition, LWT had undertaken a major exercise in rewriting and updating operational rule books with the unions, disposing of investments in subsidiary companies and generally putting our house in order. This had been considerably helped by the action taken by Margaret Thatcher in securing legislation to ban secondary picketing, which up to that time had meant that transmission of the signal from LWT carrying our programmes and advertisements could be blocked by other associated unions, thus holding LWT ro ransom. The new rules allowed us to replace outdated agreements put in place in the early days of live television, which had resulted in extortionate payments to VTR engineers. Sophisticated electronic editing procedures replaced the old system.

The process of updating the rulebooks was led by Greg Dyke, with the forceful support of Christopher Bland, who also initiated the major reconstruction of LWT's capital base. This involved both the assumption of a £70 million loan, the repayment of capital to shareholders and the creation of a special class of management shares to be allocated to key members of the management team. This enabled the company to tie in its principle creative, sales and managerial talent prior to the commencement of the franchise application process.

The management shares to be issued to the key executives had however to be paid for by them at a post-recapitalisation market price of 80p per share (50p having already been distributed to the shareholders), but would be convertible into ordinary shares in 1993, four years after the franchises had been awarded, on a multiple depending on the market price four years later at the end of 1992. The ratchet multiplier adopted would be on a one-to-one basis up to 150p, just under double the price paid by executives, with a multiple of 4 for 1 if a share price of £4.50 could be achieved. The total percentage of shares involved amounted to 2.5% of the total share capital of the company. If a value per share of £4.50 could be achieved, ie over five times the value in 1988, then the special management shares would amount to 10% of the equity of the company, but the existing shareholders would have made over five times the value of their investment.

The capital restructure required the approval of 75% of total shareholders. A succession of meetings was held with major shareholders. Despite the highly innovative nature of the incentive scheme, major shareholders such as Mercury Asset Management and Fidelity welcomed the scheme, while more conservative shareholders such as Pearl were more difficult to convince. In the event the percentage vote required was passed by a small margin.

The capital reorganisation and the introduction of the management incentive scheme provided a massive incentive for LWT to secure the renewal of its franchises at the lowest annual cost possible. There was no incentive to retain the franchises by bidding the sort of money that left a share price at 80p or even 150p.

Under the guidance of Brian Tesler LWT had achieved an enviable reputation as a programme maker, with major successes in current affairs, *Weekend World*, arts programmes with Melvyn Bragg and drama under Nick Elliott. We also had a strong sales and marketing team under Ron Miller, with some extremely talented executives. As such LWT was perceived as a difficult act to follow, but it was inevitable that there would be competition. It soon emerged that two consortia had formed to bid for the LWT franchises with some talented film and programme talent. Michael Green was the likely bidder for the Thames weekday franchise, and we had joined forces with Carlton in jointly bidding for the breakfast franchise.

We had to determine the strength of the opposition and the amount they were likely to bid for the LWT franchises. To do so involved building a model on the assumption that we were a 'green field bidder'. This indicated that an opposing bidder was likely to bid some £30 to £35 million p.a. for the franchise. Had we bid and won at this level it is unlikely that the company share price would be worth more than £1 per share and we would have a large number of dissatisfied shareholders and employees. At the time there were a number of other factors to be taken into consideration, in particular:

Would the ITC (previously called the IBA) award Carlton the weekday franchise?

If they did, could the ITC risk changing both the London franchises?

Was LWT's programme strength sufficient to justify the ITC awarding the franchises at a lower price?

Would the ITC face a judicial review if the franchise was awarded to LWT at a lower price?

At what sort of level would a lower bid be considered derisory?

These issues were debated at length in a final meeting of the LWT's franchise team at Hever Castle, under close security conditions. Any bid at more than £35 million would clearly not be in our long-term interest. We decided to take a calculated risk, based on Carlton winning the weekday franchise and LWT's programme and other strengths being sufficiently convincing to persuade the ITC to award LWT its franchise at a much lower figure, risking a possible judicial review. It was not an easy decision for the ITC.

I proposed a bid of £7 million, which was supported by Greg Dyke, the lowest bid that could be considered respectable, although a slightly higher one was ultimately agreed at £7.8 million, supported both by Greg and Christopher. The risk was well taken, and LWT's franchise was renewed, despite being much lower than the competitor's bid of £35 million per annum. However I believe it was a close thing, because subsequent indications were that if the failed competitor had asked for a judicial review, it might have been very difficult for the ITC to refuse it, thus opening a whole new can of worms.

The joint bid LWT and Carlton put in for the breakfast franchise was also won, albeit at a much higher level.

Would such an outcome have been achieved under a different chairman and chief executive? I doubt it. Would we have had the determination to undertake the radical capital restructuring and take on the significant loan obligations and the repayments of capital to shareholders? I think not. It was a once-in-a lifetime opportunity, for which most credit must go to Christopher Bland - a major beneficiary of the scheme.

The award of the franchise had an immediate effect on LWT's shares, which gradually increased to £4.50 over the next four years. This gave the holders of the management shares an entitlement to four shares for each one owned. It was a major success all round.

For the first time in my life I actually felt moderately well off. The French gypsy fortune teller's prophesy had come true, though I had to wait more than 30 years. It was a final triumph for LWT.

The LWT franchise winning team, 1991: Tony Cohen, Barry Cox, PM, Brian Tesler,
Sir Christopher Bland, Greg Dyke, Tony Kay, Neil Canetty-Clarke

CHAPTER 12

OTHER FINANCIAL INTERESTS
1970S – 1990s

At LWT I was not entirely happy with my salary. John Freeman had many talents, but he was extremely careful and very modest with his own company expenses. This was reflected in the company's remuneration policy and in the level of salaries paid to LWT senior staff and directors. In this he was originally aided by Lord Campbell of Eskan, who was not known for his generosity. Although we had a first-class pension scheme, remuneration levels at LWT were below those paid by the other ITV contractors, a source of some disappointment.

Accordingly, when in the mid 1970s I was asked to become a non-executive director of Johnson & Jourgenson, a manufacturer of plastic containers for the pharmaceutical industry, I was happy that John Freeman was prepared for me to do so, as well as taking up non-executive directorships in other companies. With a mortgage and school fees to pay the extra income was very necessary. Some years later Johnson and Jourgenson was listed on the alternative investment market (AIM), having separated its property holdings from its manufacturing activities. It was subsequently sold to Metal Box at a significant premium.

I also joined the board of Westminster and Country Properties, a small quoted property development company, in which an old friend, David Parks, was the principal shareholder. He needed to strengthen his representation on the board to balance some very talented executives. The Parks family shareholding was subsequently sold to a consortium put together by Robert Brear, chaired by Sir Peter Parker, and the name changed to Arcadian International, which carried out a number of international developments of hotel and golf club resorts. Even after the sale I remained a non-executive director for ten years.

Less successful was my directorship of Company of Designers, a group of architectural practices which was launched on to the AIM market by an energetic and charismatic chairman who had put together a group of architectural practices across the country with the object of being one of the largest design companies in the UK. Unfortunately this left the company highly geared, and in the late 1980s, with a sudden reduction of commissions, it became dangerously exposed. This led to the resignation of the chairman and my taking his place, albeit with considerable reluctance. Not a happy situation!

We tried to persuade the banks to convert bank loans to equity, unfortunately without success. In order to avoid wholesale redundancy, arrangements were made with the principal architects' practices to buy back their businesses as part of the company's move into administration. In retrospect I don't believe a stock exchange listing is the right place for a business depending on individual personal talent such as architecture.

In the mid 1970s I had became a Lloyds underwriter, initially with some good and some indifferent syndicates, through a members' agent,

R F Kirshaw, to whom I was introduced by Charles Stuart-Monteith. From the outset I insisted on taking out a stop loss insurance, which served me well in the nineties when I was saved from serious losses. In the mid 1980s I used to compare my results with those of Melvyn Bragg at LWT. His results were always better than mine, to the extent that I eventually transferred my underwriting to Melvyn's agent, Robert Hiscox, who subsequently took most of his names out of Lloyds in 1999. Despite the losses in 1993 my overall results from Lloyds just about broke even after stop loss and tax relief and provided help with school fees in the early years.

I was extremely fortunate to have joined LWT in 1969, when ITV had a monopoly of advertising revenue and with it a commitment to produce high-quality news, arts, documentaries, current affairs, drama and entertainment programmes, making a major contribution to the Exchequer through a levy on turnover and subsequently on profits. Fortunately that monopoly remained largely unchallenged up to my retirement and the takeover of LWT by Granada in 1994.

I was also privileged to work with some extremely talented directors, executives and programme makers. Apparently Peter Mandelson worked in the Current Affairs Department from 1982 to 1985. I can't remember ever meeting him, but I believe he and a number of my LWT colleagues, John Birt, Greg Dyke, Melvyn Bragg and Barry Cox, were members of a clique which was partly responsible for Tony Blair's election to the leadership of the Labour Party and subsequently to the premiership.

In recent years the proliferation of television channels has led to the inevitable dilution of audience and advertising revenue and the creation of the internet, necessitating the consolidation of the ITV companies into a much smaller entity and the reduction of ITV's public service obligations. This has made it very difficult for ITV to compete with the BBC and BSkyB for talent and sporting rights, the BBC having an income from the licence fee roughly three and a half times that of ITV's advertising revenue. ITV would however be really sunk if the BBC were funded by advertising in what has become a very competitive market.

CHAPTER 13

AN EVENTFUL RETIREMENT
1993 AND AFTER

Retiring from LWT at 60 in 1993 opened up a new world for me. Having benefited from the franchise auction and the sale of a significant percentage of my LWT shares, I determined to improve my French and my tennis and teach myself to paint, something I had always wanted to do. There was a three-month trip to South Africa, and moving down to Cap d'Antibes for two years helped enormously with my painting; the colours and the scents there are quite unique. The move led to two one-man exhibitions of my paintings in Cork Street, where I sold a few pictures.

Unfortunately these periods away also contributed to the breakdown of my marriage. In the years before retirement, for a number of reasons, my relationship with Edmée had not been easy. I was tempted into an affair with a voluptuous creature, and unfortunately this led to the parting of the ways.

I took off to South Africa, where I was generously entertained by Michael Shurey and the Japhets and went on a number of game and fishing safaris, including white-water rafting on the Zambezi. On my return to the UK I was helped by my brother Paddy, who allowed me to stay in one of his houses in Highworth. Paddy, an exceptionally successful and generous brother, is well known for his involvement in Formula 1 motor racing. Probably not so well known is his remarkable expertise in renovating Georgian houses. He is a real perfectionist.

Exhibition at the Osborne Gallery

Whitewater rafting on the Zambezi, 1994

Ascot 1995, with Aileen Hay and Patricia Tallon

In 1994 I bought out some of the minority shareholding in Sunspot Tours, a company started by my son-in-law, Martin Bugeja. Additionally I subscribed in new equity in the company, together with Leon Page and Nigel Cole, who joined the board as directors with myself as chairman.

Sunspot had had a couple of unsatisfactory years, but from 1994, under Martin's direction, results began to improve, helped by the input from Leon, an industry veteran, and Nigel on the marketing side. The company has now become an outstanding success, with the majority of the non-family shareholders having been bought in so that the company is now 75% owned by Martin and his talented team of female directors. My investment in Sunspot turned out to be one of the best I have ever made.

On retirement from LWT I stayed on as a trustee of the pension scheme, which had a substantial actuarial surplus after the takeover of LWT in 1994 by Granada. The scheme was subsequently merged with the Granada scheme and I then had to step down as a trustee. Two years later I became aware that the substantial commercial property portfolio and the high-yielding government gilts, investments carefully built up over the years, had been sold and the proceeds invested in equities, wholly inappropriate for a mature fund. Furthermore, based on over-optimistic actuarial assumptions of future income, no company contributions were being made by Granada.

I was appalled. Since 1996 I have been writing to successive Granada (non-ITV) chairmen concerning the lack of company contributions, the inappropriate investment policy and the ever-increasing pension fund deficit, which has not been helped by the increasing longevity of members. Under Sir Peter Burt's chairmanship my efforts finally resulted in an additional payment into the fund of £300m. It was too little, too late.

One of my minor criticisms has been that there was no independent chairman of the trustees. With over 96% of the scheme members being pensioners or deferred pensioners, this is unacceptable and requires radical action, both to eliminate the deficit and and appoint a new chairman. If the ITV scheme were to be wound up tomorrow, the deficit would be in the region of £1.5 billion.

With Jamie Blandford and brother Patrick at my 70th birthday party

Beatrice (right) with Henry and Gloria Bathurst at my 70th

I considered suing the Granada Pension Fund trustees, but was advised by litigation lawyers that as I had not yet personally suffered a loss it would be difficult to do so.

Apart from some charity work for the local hospital in Swindon, I have been serving as trustee to two landed estates. With the first, the Denbigh Estate at Newnham Paddox, I agreed to become a trustee after several years of persuasion by Rollo, on condition that he would always support me in the event of disagreement.

Rollo and I never had a disagreement. Sadly he died in 1995. He was a wonderful friend with immense charm, and his early death was a serious loss for his family and all friends. Despite some headaches, they have helped to fill my leisure time in retirement and each has brought its own reward. Preserving an agricultural estate with relatively low return and the cash flow requirements of young families will always involve potential conflicts in providing adequate income while maintaining a sufficient capital base for future generations.

In my working life I have been extremely fortunate to work with and know some extraordinarily talented individuals, from my very early years at GEC with Arnold Weinstock and Kenneth Bond at LWT through the early years with Frank Muir, Jimmy Hill, John Bromley, Vic Gardiner, Cyril Bennett and Roger Appleton and in later years John Birt, Brian Walden, David Montagu, Michael Grade, John Freeman, Brian Tesler, Sir Christopher Bland, Melvyn Bragg, Nick Elliot, Barry Cox and Greg Dyke, most of whom have achieved considerable success in other fields as well as with LWT.

In recent years I have also enjoyed the company of a number of very talented individuals, writers and journalists, including Harry Chapman Pincher and Sir Max Hastings, whose sensible and well-informed articles in the *FT* and *Daily Mail* have challenged so much of the perceived wisdom of the day. I have also enjoyed the company of my fishing and shooting friends, notably Johnny Kimberley, Gerald Ward, Jeremy Paxman, Peter Inchcape, Sir George Russell, Sir Richard Dashwood, Freddy Tulloch and Cristo Headford, mainly beside the River Kennet or in the shooting field.

One of the factors which motivated me during my working life was the fear of dependency in old age without adequate resources. This made me very determined to succeed financially, but it also coloured my attitude when recruiting executives. I wanted people who were not too financially secure and had the determination to complete whatever difficult task was required, even if it meant working through the night to do so.

I was discussing this with Rupert Soames on a fishing trip to

With my brother Paddy, 2005

the River Figgio in Norway in 2005. He is the grandson of Winston Churchill, and like me had worked for GEC under Arnold Weinstock and was the chief executive of a publicly-quoted company, a generator hire business called Aggreco. He suggested I would not therefore have employed him! He was of course right, but I would have made a very serious mistake in not doing so because he has built up Aggreco to be a remarkable success story with the share price going from £3 in 2005 to over £23 in the last few months. What a shame I didn't invest, because I then thought the shares were too expensive – they yielded less than 1% and were selling at a price which was 29 times that of the previous year's profit! A serious misjudgement on my part.

With my brothers at Boodles, 1999 – left to right, Paddy, PM, Charles and John

CLOSING
THOUGHTS

Retirement gives one time at last to ponder, to contemplate and to review. Looking back on my life, I find there are some topics which are particularly close to my heart. Here are some of them.

RELIGION & RACE

 ❧

I was brought up by parents with a strong religious belief, and Christianity and Catholicism were drummed into me and my brothers from a very early age. This was reinforced by being sent to Hodder, the preparatory school for Stonyhurst, at the age of 10 on our return from Ireland in 1943. Both my junior school and Stonyhurst were predominantly run by Jesuits with a small number of lay teachers, some of whom had been brought out of retirement during the war years. In those days the school régime was extremely strict, with physical punishment being liberally dispensed. The concept was that 'to spare the rod was to spoil the child'. We certainly were not spoiled! My religious teaching was extremely dogmatic, with little opportunity for discussion or challenge. There was no room for argument.

We were taught that only Catholics would go to Heaven and that we were exceptionally privileged to be brought up as Catholics and to attend such a school. I suppose this could have made us all feel good, but it did not. What about all the other religious groups? Did they not have an equal right to heavenly bliss? What about the millions of people who had lived and died in the thousands of years before Christ? Why should such a natural thing as sex be sinful - surely it is an essential element of life on Earth?

While these unanswered questions remained, it was difficult not to acknowledge that the intelligence and intellectual qualifications of the Stonyhurst Jesuits were vastly superior to my own, and accordingly their beliefs should be accepted without question.

Up to the time of my retirement from LWT in 1993 I had not spent much time or thought much about Catholic belief or other religions. Since then, during holidays in Egypt, Mexico, South Africa, Jordan, Thailand and India, I have become more closely aware of other cultures and religions. This has brought home to me the similarities, rather than the differences, between the beliefs and the doctrines of most of the world's major religions. One of the earliest known religious beliefs belongs to ancient Egypt, when as long ago as 3000 BC there was a strong belief in life after death, coupled with a belief in one god, Amon. Much of Christian belief reflects a striking similarity with such early faiths.

Most major religions embody sets of beliefs which provide rules for people to live in harmony with each other. All recognise the existence of a major force for life on our planet and seek to provide a meaning for life. Modern scientific evidence shows that life has existed on Earth for thousands of millions of years, mankind for several million years and most known religions for a miniscule percentage of that time. Science now tells us that time and space are infinite and that the 5000 years of our planet's recorded history is only a microsecond in the history of time. The concept of infinite time and space tests our comprehension and understanding; we now know that there are millions of galaxies, stars and planets, stretching over billions of light years. It is difficult to imagine that there are no other planets among them which are also capable of sustaining life. Where does that leave religious belief?

Is God another name for a supreme life force which generates life on Earth, recognised by different names and practices by most major religions, each of which adheres to different dogmas, practices and codes of human conduct? If we examine these beliefs and compare the main strictures of each religion, it is surprising to find so much common ground. It is likely that 70% of the basic beliefs are similar if not identical for the world's major religions and that the existence of these religions reflects mankind's search for a reason for his existence and a purpose in life.

Different religions seek to translate the concept of life force into more easily identified and understandable beliefs. They also recognise mankind's desire for security and rules to allow communities to live without conflict with each other, providing common purpose and a cohesive potential for unity.

Membership of a particular religion is almost invariably an accident of birth rather than of choice, and through the generations it provides a source of continuity and cohesion between family, ethnic and tribal groups. In the purest sense most religions are a source of good, helping to enhance the lives of their members, providing compassion and support through their lives and hope and consolation in old age.

When such ideologies, relying as they do on an almighty, all-powerful deity, are taken to extremes and combined with ethnic and tribal differences, the result can be the most appalling inhumanity, cruelty and barbarism against the non believer - Christian against Moslem, Protestant against Catholic, Muslim against Hindu, Suni against Shi-ite. In fact some of the worst atrocities were committed in the crusades in the 11th and 12th Century by Christians against Muslims in the so called 'Holy War'. The atrocities committed in the name of religion have been quite horrendous by modern thinking, such as the inquisition in the 16th century and the modern-day killing of the innocents, as in the destruction of the Twin Towers in the USA.

A degree of religious freedom was evident in India in the 18th century, when there was a tolerance between the major religions, Hindu, Muslim and Buddhist, and their religious sects. This only erupted into conflict with the partition of India in 1946 and the significant exodus of Muslims from India and Hindus from Pakistan.

The advance of scientific knowledge and improved communications in recent years have called to question the fundamental basis on which religious belief has been established and the disparity in the living standards of populations in the industrialised developed world and those of the developing world. The massive growth in the world population in recent years has alerted us to the need for conservation of natural resources, for which there will be an ever-increasing demand in years to come.

The population of the world did not reach one billion until 1804; today it is almost seven billion. Inevitably this will give rise to conflict for scarce resources between communities and nations.

Very few religions, with the possible exception of Buddhism, appear to give much recognition to the dependence of the human race on other life forms and the interdependence and complexity of the plants, micro-organisms, insects and other life forms on which humanity and all other animal life depends. Mankind has existed on this planet for hundreds of thousands of years, possibly millions. What differentiates us from the other creatures is the development of our brain, which has enabled us to increase and multiply. The development of medicines, science and industry has helped us to survive. Physically, however, we are not much different from other living creatures, so we are equally susceptible to earthquakes, floods, famine, droughts and other catastrophes.

Religious dogmatism largely rejects the extensive knowledge that science has brought us in the last hundred years. Much of scientific research is at odds with the many of the fundamental concepts and beliefs of most major religions.

Did God create man or did man create God?

There is clearly a force which has resulted in the creation of an extremely complex world environment over millions of years. Animals, fish, plants, insects and other organisms have developed in a bewildering, complex and independent way.

Earlier religions which included the worship of the sun were not far off the mark in many respects, as the sun provides the energy which creates life and the climate which regulates growth and reproduction on our planet. All major religions recognise this creative life force, personifying it with different names – God, Allah, Buddha, Shiva.

It is possible that there are many other planetary systems which could sustain similar life forms with their own suns, which will continue to exist once our sun has burned out in several billion years' time.

The infinity of time and space makes human life on Planet Earth appear parochial and unimportant. Our brief life cycle, our fight for survival, the pursuit of fulfilment, of recognition, of material wealth and happiness, all seem inconsequential by comparison with the scale of the universe.

With an ever-increasing world population, extreme fundamental religious beliefs can pose serious dangers to society. If we reject religious belief, what should we do to replace it? What shall we tell our children? How do we instil a sense of morality and responsibility in succeeding generations? How do we ensure the survival of our children and grandchildren, and live in harmony with our fellow beings and other earthly life forms? Is there still justification for faith schools, where educational standards may be extremely high, but which may produce religious extremists?

What of the institutions and cultures which are part of the Christian heritage, the judicial – property ownership, local government and the whole infrastructure of society in the western world? The increase in the population in recent years is putting serious demands on world resources and creating massive pollution of natural resources. In the 21st century we face future significant growth in world population. There is intense competition for the world's finite resources, increased overcrowding of our cities and pressure on government infrastructure, education and health systems. Western cultures now have to cope with immigration from the underdeveloped countries. People are moving from the southern hemisphere into the affluent western economies bringing with them different, often dogmatic, beliefs and customs.

Christianity is also an integral part of our evolving social system, a system which has brought security, infrastructure and property rights to our nation and its inhabitants for almost a thousand years.

In the west we have been extremely privileged in the exploitation of the earth's natural resources. In the UK we have benefited from the Industrial Revolution and the building up of empire in the 18th and 19th centuries. Although in the last century the financial strength of the UK has been heavily depleted by two world wars, North Sea oil has made a major contribution to our economy in the last 50 years. Unfortunately this has allowed our manufacturing industry to decline. Since 1997 the UK Government has allowed the cost of running the country's public services, in particular welfare, to absorb an ever-increasing percentage of our gross domestic product, with a massive increase in the number of public service employees. These, together with improvements in world communication systems and over-generous welfare benefits, have made the UK a magnet for underprivileged immigrants from the deprived and underdeveloped countries, who have brought with them different ethics and cultures, to the detriment of the indigenous population.

How can this be redressed? With great difficulty. Already a large percentage of births in our cities are to mothers not born in the UK. Our over-liberal and bureaucratic legal system is not equipped to cope with the influx of criminals from Eastern Europe and Northern Africa. EU Human Rights Legislation prevents us from deporting robbers, rapists and murderers and other dangerous immigrants clogging up our already overstretched legal system. This is not helped by our left-leaning judiciary, which through Legal Aid profits from the protection of criminals preventing their deportation.

We need to introduce legislation to get rid of the Human Rights Act and to limit immigration to those with a sound command of the English language and a required skill restricting the time allowed for students and guest workers to be strictly enforced by a reorganised immigration service.

In the last ten years the Government has been responsible for a massive growth in bureaucracy, providing a multilingual service in an ever-expanding welfare state. This has to stop.

FISHING –
A LIFELONG PASSION

EARLY DAYS

Fishing became a passion for me at a very early age, probably from the age of ten, when I was sent to prep school in Lancashire. Up to that time we had been living at Poplar Vale in Monaghan, Ireland, and had not had the opportunity to fish as we were too young, despite all the fishing in the area and with my father based in Iraq and in the Middle East Land Force in Egypt.

However in 1944 he was briefly posted to Lytham St Annes on the Lancashire coast and he arranged to take us three boys fishing at a reservoir nearby, where he taught us to cast a fly. The fact that we caught a number of trout must have meant that the reservoir was very full of fish, because I think we were pretty incompetent, but my brother John and I were hooked for life.

Once I had started at Stonyhurst later that year, fishing became a regular addiction, with the school having ancient fishing rights on the River Hodder. As mentioned above, a supportive rugby coach, Father Tranmar, uniquely allowed me to forego cricket and spend two hours each week by the river instead. At that time I was in both the school boxing and rugby teams. He commented that it was better that I was on the river than disrupting the cricket game, for which I had little competence!

In 1945 my father was posted to Melksham, near Devizes in Wiltshire, where we were introduced to coarse fishing on a local canal with an extensive lock system. In addition to the perch, roach and bream, there was an occasional monster pike. There was a time when John and I had both hooked pike in a lock and brother John fell in. Neither of the hooked fish were landed, but John, luckily, was saved.

Another fishing event occurred during a summer holiday in Ireland, when my brother Charles and I were staying with our Aunt Anne at her house in Monaghan, Hillside. We were taken fishing by my bachelor uncle John, but before we were allowed to go to the river we had several hours of casting lessons on the tennis lawn. We were also shown how to make a wagtail spinner out of leather to spin for pike (with beads, hooks, swivels and painted eyes). The spinning reels then available were quite difficult to use compared to modern fixed-spool reels, which had not by then been invented, but we eventually got the hang of them. One afternoon we got thirteen pike, which we brought back in triumph to be photographed in the tennis court. I cannot remember if we had them to eat, but I suspect not.

It was not until my parents had retired to Marlow in 1960 that I had the opportunity of fishing a chalk stream, an eye-opening experience. The mother of one of my parents' neighbours, Dr Kidd, had a charming mill house on the River Dever at Barton Stacey, and I was taken there by their son, Malcolm. The river was narrow and crystal clear and the trout all clearly visible to us, as we were to them. Fortunately, with constant perseverance and a little bit of luck, I finished up with two trout of 1½ and 2 lbs, much to the annoyance of my host, who caught nothing. At that time the river was quite overgrown and hardly fished.

The mill and its 20 acres were sold by the Kidds in the late 1960s for £20,000, which seemed a lot of money at the time. It has changed hands several times since and is now owned by Sally Morrison, an accomplished greyhound breeder. I would have loved to have owned Bransbury Mill, with its kingfishers and other wild birds and its own little private shoot. Sadly I did not have that sort of money then for the major expenditure required to modernise it. Instead, as mentioned above, I bought a run-down 17th century pub in the Hambledon valley and spent two years restoring it at the weekends, which did not allow much time for fishing.

At about that time I was offered and took a Saturday rod to fish the Loddon on the Duke of Wellington's estate at Stratfield Saye. The fishing was split into six rotating beats, each rod being able to fish one day a week on a different beat. Each beat had its own fishing hut, and you knew you had the beat to yourself for the whole day and that nobody else would have fished there that day.

The Loddon is not a classic chalk stream but it rises in chalk – above Sherfield on Loddon – and the upper river is clear and fast-flowing with overgrown banks which are difficult to access. Where the river went through the Stratfield Saye Estate a number of fast runs were joined by deep holes containing some extremely large fish. Each rod was allowed to bring a guest on his nominated day, with dry fly being obligatory until July 1st. In the early 1960s there was a reasonable hatch of fly, with an exceptional mayfly hatch at the beginning of June. Since then the fly life has reduced significantly, although I understand there is still a modest mayfly hatch, and the rules have been somewhat changed to allow nymph fishing before July.

Over the years the Loddon became an excellent place to

entertain family and fishing friends, and in 1979 I bought a cottage in Wildmoor, close to Sherfield-on-Loddon, to be near the fishing at weekends. This thatched cottage was originally two up and two down, the only bathroom being on the ground floor. Having sold the house in Addison Avenue and bought a house in Fulham, it was a delightful place to spend weekends.

On summer evenings we would hunt crayfish. We had found some old metal rings, which turned out to be from crayfish nets. We re-covered them in netting, baited them with an old oily fish or rabbit and lowered them into the neck of a deep pool. The rings were then left for about 30 minutes before being raised to the surface, and if you were lucky there would be a number of crayfish on the top of the net, which could then be tipped into a bucket and the ring placed back into the river. The crayfish were then taken back to the cottage to be cooked for five minutes and eaten – really delicious!

When the cottage was sold in 1986 the crayfish rings were brought back to our new house in Saxon Hall in Lambourne, but they have never been seen again.

I kept my rod on the Loddon until 2004, when I passed it on to my son Markus, having found some fishing on the Kennet closer to my house in Hannington Wick. One of my guests in the early years on the Loddon was Johnny Kimberley, who had previously only been deep sea fishing and had never cast a fly before. He was a great enthusiast and took to fly fishing like a duck to water. The following year he took me to another beat on the Kennet, owned by Gerald Ward, at Chilton Foliat. The Kennet was much clearer and faster than the Loddon, although Gerald did not operate the beat rotation system which was so attractive at Stratfield Saye.

Trout fishing was and still is my first love when the water is gin clear, and with careful observation you can see the dimple of a feeding fish in the water. The challenge of placing the fly oh so gently six inches ahead of the rise in the face of a downstream breeze, and the excitement of seeing the fish move to the fly – will he take it, or is he just looking? Just looking! Cast again – he looks again and rejects it. Wait a few minutes. This time change the fly – and this time he takes. It is a good fish, he is running downstream – let him go, keep the pressure on, but not too much – keep him away from the weed – gradually he turns, but he is off again, the final dash downstream, then back up into the net!

In the last few years I have been lucky enough to have a rod on a particularly beautiful stretch of the Kennet at Chilton Foliat, on the Eastridge Estate owned until recently by Sir Seaton Wills. Here the river runs fast and clear, and the occasional slow deep stretches hold some monster fish. This water has provided me and my guests with some excellent sport.

Salmon

Some years earlier Johnny Kimberley, whom I had introduced to trout fishing, decided that he would like to catch slightly bigger fish, and persuaded a number of his friends in the House of Lords to allow us to fish their private rivers in Scotland. This resulted in some most enjoyable trips to Scotland to fish the Lochy, Thurso, Tweed and Spey. Initially a typical trip involved two to four rods with assorted wives or girlfriends, generally staying at a small fishing hotel. We enjoyed some extremely interesting trips to Alec Douglas Home's beat at Coldstream on the Tweed, and on the Carron and the Lochy.

The following year Johnny met Ginger Seafield (Earl of Seafield), who had not one beat but four on the Spey, two with lodges. The principal beat, Castle Grant Beat 1, was let with Kinveachy Lodge, which could accommodate a party of 20. It was a wonderful opportunity to organise a number of big fishing parties, at which Johnny was expert and a brilliant host. The drawback was that the beat was for six rods and was some 15 miles from the lodge. It was not ideal if you were a keen fisherman, but great fun if you enjoyed a good party with a little fishing on the side!

Johnny's parties always included a wide variety of different characters – authors, newspaper editors, PR agents, property developers, bankers, air marshals and media personnel (I suppose this is me!) and the odd MP, estate agent or night club owner, with assorted wives and girlfriends. Notable guests at Kinveachy included

In a fishing party with Johnny Kimberley on the Spey, 1996

My sons Markus and Alexis with their first salmon, River Beauly 1995

A salmon taken from the Gaula, 2010

With a fresh salmon from the Hofsa, Iceland

Freddie Forsyth, Bertie Denham, Max Hastings, Nigel Corbally Stourton, Geoffrey Clifton Brown, John Fenston, Sir Roddy Brinckman, Roger Poulter, Peter Reichwald, Henrietta and Sebastian Thewes, Timothy Dalton, Jeremy Paxman and Brian Basham.

Not all the guests fished with the same diligence. Because of the distance to the river, few went out in the evening and there was usually a full house for dinner, which tended to be great fun and extremely boisterous. From 11 am most mornings Johnny held court in the fishing hut with the gillie, John Thompson, to start the day's alcoholic marathon with Bertie Denham's White Ladies. Not surprisingly, one year he had 23 days' salmon fishing without catching one.

Johnny was a wonderful host, putting together great parties with lots of different characters. It was most entertaining with his mixture of family and friends. They were always great fun – that was the good thing, but the bad thing was the bar bill! He generally took three separate weeks at Castle Grant and if he had a full complement of guests it probably paid for his own fishing. Sometimes it didn't!

In recent years I have been going up in September to Castle Grant Beat 2, where guests stay at Inverallen House, the ex-factor's house, which has been converted into a very friendly and comfortable lodge with six double bedrooms all with bathrooms, organised by Peter Reichwald, one of Johnny's old fishing friends. The food is invariably first class and the river full of fish, albeit reluctant takers. The head gillie, Lionel, is certainly first rate – he is extremely diplomatic and efficient in organising and encouraging the rods. Although catch and release is largely the rule now, with all hen fish being returned, a silver cock fish may be kept. Additionally the estate generously gives two sides of smoked salmon for every

The Hafalonsa River, Iceland: Nigel Corbally-Stourton, Roger Poulter, Victoria Sheffield, self, gillies

salmon returned to the river up to a maximum of six (this is one way of making catch and release acceptable).

In May each year for the past 30 years or so I have been lucky enough to fish the Dee at Banchory, one of the most productive beats on the river, with Edwin and Tristan Bailey. Invery, the beat just below Banchory, has a mile of double bank fishing and half a mile of single bank and is extremely attractive and easily waded. We used to stay at Banchory Lodge Hotel, close to the river, but in recent years we have been staying at Raemoor Hotel, some two miles outside Banchory. Unfortunately over the last twenty years the early runs of fish have disappeared and the number of May fish have been disappointing. However catches have improved in the last year or so and 2010 saw a dozen fish caught in the Invery beat in the first week in May, probably due to the skill of two very professional guests, Ralph Percy and David Hoare. I caught two fish, but they weren't very big.

Elsewhere salmon fishing has taken me to Norway and Iceland, the Hafelonsa and Hofsa, two rivers on the north east coast. The first was run by Roxtons, and here I was first introduced to a hitched and skated fly, the riffle hitch. The upper pools involved climbing down by rope to the river bed. The water was so clear that you could see fish lying deep in the pools, and with the help of the guide you could experience the fish coming up and taking the flies from the surface.

The Hofsa was run very efficiently by Edda Helgeson. Both complete river systems run through deep gorges into shallow treeless valleys and down to smooth estuaries; it is a landscape full of long shingle-covered river banks, full of tiny wild flowers and the strained sound of sea birds.

Sea fishing and 'big game'

Fishing for bonefish is fly fishing in salt water, and it has become an addiction for me in the last ten years. It involves casting a lure to fish coming on to the flats in search of crabs and shrimps. The lure looks very much like a traditional salmon fly, but with two eyes. The sport takes you on to shallow tidal waters in a number of exciting locations, including the Bahamas, Cuba and the Seychelles. Sometimes you wade up to your knees or sometimes cast from the front of a skiff, generally with two fishermen sharing a guide, whose eyes generally spot the fish earlier than the rods. I have enjoyed several memorable trips to Cuba at the Jardinas de la Rena, Andros at Kalamanie Cay, Bahamas, Alphonse Island in the Seychelles and Des Roche, also in the Seychelles, the latter three being the best organised and most comfortable.

Bonefish are all muscle, and are noted as one of the strongest fighting fish. It is wise to have several hundred yards of backing, as a even a 3 lb fish can take 100 yards of line in its first run. The biggest bone I have caught was in Andros, where I hooked a 10 lb fish which took 300 yards of backing from my reel in two long runs. I was down to the last few yards when eventually I managed to recover some line. It took some 30 minutes before the fish was beside the boat, my guide having sat down and lit a cigarette! Unfortunately the fish was bleeding by the time it came out of the water and I am afraid the guide decided he would prefer to have it for his supper than to see the sharks take it.

Although I haven't been deep sea fishing very often, it has a special fascination because of the potential size of the prey. Sea fishing trips are remembered by long periods of inactivity, followed by minutes of pandemonium and chaos.

My sea fishing started with fishing off a pier with handlines on the south coast, using a paternoster and several lugworms catapulted by rod into the sea below. I remember a trip to Devon in the 1970s when little was caught. The combination of a heavy swell and the smell of 'rubby dubby' (a bag of rotten fish) put over the side to attract the sharks resulted in the whole party throwing up and the fishing trip being cut short!

The bonefish flats, Alphonse Island, Seychelles

An eight-pound bonefish safely landed

With a ten-pound bonefish

My next major fishing trip was the result of an introduction by Johnny Kimberley to Roger Levitt, said to be an extremely successful insurance broker. Roger was a human dynamo with piercing blue eyes who was keen to expand the circle of his business acquaintances. Having established my interest in fishing, he invited Freddie Forsyth and me to come shark fishing off Salcombe in Devon. He drove us down in his Bentley Continental at speeds of up to 140 mph!

We caught a number of sharks, some of reasonable size, and enjoyed a pleasant and amusing weekend together before being whisked back to London at equal speed in the Bentley. I am afraid Roger took people for a ride in more ways than one, though at that time we had no reason to question his integrity as he had sold 5% of his company to a major insurance company for £7 million and added an ex-Bank of England director to his board. This did much to counter my initial prejudice against his forceful sales approach. Luckily I never invested with him, unlike some of Johnny Kimberley's friends, who lost a great deal of money!

Some years later on a family holiday in Hawaii we went marlin fishing off the big island, having chartered a boat for the afternoon. We briefly hooked a sizeable fish after an hour or so, only to see it seconds later tailing perpendicularly 100 yards behind the boat and throwing the line and bait high into the air. This whetted our appetite, and we chartered a fishing boat for two more days. First we had to catch the livebait, yellowfin tuna of four or five kilos each. After a couple of days of disappointing fishing we hooked and lost another big fish and ended up having to eat the tuna for supper.

In 1992 I was lucky enough to be invited to join my brother Paddy on Lizard Island on the Australian Great Barrier Reef for the

Lexus Marling Fishing Championship, having obtained some highly discounted club class air fares. It was the cumulation of an extensive trip Down Under.

Paddy had arranged to stay with a group of friends at Lizard Island, which was closer to the Great Barrier Reef than Cooktown, where the majority of the competing boats were based. This gave

With my sons Alexis and Markus and grandson Max at the Manor

us a useful advantage. He had an excellent South African captain, Dennis, an accomplished deep-sea fisherman. With four heavily-baited rods and an agreed order for handling any strikes, we were off to a flying start. Under the competition rules only one fisherman could touch the rod when the fish had been hooked, with the rod being slotted into the base of the fighting seat and the reel secured by a clip on each side of the fighting chair. When the fish hit the bait the captain would stop the engine. The fisherman, if not already in the chair, would climb into it and be handed the appropriate rod secured by clips on either side. This gave the fish time to swallow the bait.

The captain would accelerate to strike the fish, with the fisherman holding the rod tightly with both hands. He was then in for the fight of his life. We had a number of strikes on the first day, with me taking two of them. I first caught a 250 lb shark and then a 600 lb marlin, which was tagged and released.

Playing the fish involved quite a lot of skill, mainly by the captain. When the fish ran the captain reversed after it, and when it came towards the boat he accelerated so that it was always in manageable control and kept on the shortest possible line until it could be brought to the boat for measuring and tagging. Catching and playing fish is down to the skill of the captain rather than the fisherman in the fighting chair.

This became evident again to me in February 2011 in the Maldives, when I chartered a boat for an afternoon's deep sea fishing, sharing with an attractive Russian couple. I was lucky enough that the one strike of the afternoon was on my watch. However, getting into the fighting chair involved an untimely eviction of its blonde Russian occupant!

My five-year-old grandson Max with a
trout from the Kennet

Once in the chair I realised I had a monster on the line. Even using the pump action which had proved so effective on the Great Barrier Reef it was almost impossible to get line back on the reel. Instead of helping me to reel in by reversing the boat towards the fish, the captain tried to protect my hands, helping me put on a pair of gloves.

Up to that point, because of the weight of the fish, recovery of the line had been extremely slow. I have never been attached to anything quite so large. Once the second glove was on I was suddenly able to retrieve line – to find that the fish had thrown the hook. Having had it on for some twenty minutes I was tired but disappointed that putting on the gloves to protect my fingers probably reduced the pressure on the fish, allowing it to shake off the hook. Was it a marlin, a tuna or a monster shark? We will never known. It is always the big ones that get away!

DAYS WITH DOG & GUN

❦

I was introduced to shooting in Ireland at a very early age. In the early 1940s, when my father was home on leave from Iraq, he would take us shooting rabbits at Poplar Vale. None of us children was old enough to use a gun, but we enjoyed traipsing around the woods in search of rabbits, very few of which got shot by my father, whose eyesight was not too good. His family had enjoyed shoots in the 1930s, with grouse and duck being the main quarry, as the family leased a grouse moor very close to the borders. Later, at school in England and during a holiday in Ireland, I remember being taken duck flighting by my uncle John with his devoted spaniel.

Back in England, when my father was the CO of the RAF hospital in Ely, I was loaned an old 12 bore and a .22 rifle and started shooting in earnest. The quarry was mainly pigeons and rabbits, with the odd invitation from a local landowner to shoot partridges in my father's place. The shoot, just outside Ely, was in rich fenland and the guns were placed in deep ditches crossing the farm. The wild partridges were driven and flew low and fast over the guns, rather like grouse. Not surprisingly I didn't hit many.

Some time before, we had been introduced to clay pigeon shooting by my uncle John Tolhurst, who had a farm outside Shoeburyness. This was a useful way to enable us to get the hang of shooting at a moving target.

On their retirement in the early 1960s, my parents bought a house just outside Marlow where my father had been given part time work as a locum. Here he became a proficient gardener, specialising in roses, despite never having gardened in his life before. Marlow became the family base for over 20 years. It was a pretty house with a large garden within walking distance of the town and the River Thames; a very practical house, but not as large as we should have liked.

After the family moved to Marlow shooting invitations tended to be more limited, and I decided to start a small shoot locally in the woods owned by the Mash family in Little Marlow. Despite a lot of hard work and help in constructing release pens it was not a success, and convinced me that running a successful shoot has to be done professionally and not by part-time amateurs. It also needs the right topography, with the right mixture of game crops and woodland.

In the early 60s I joined a small rough shoot in Sussex, where the father of a girlfriend, Nicola Hemmingway, had a gun. We shot over land owned by a farmer, John Bromhead, and some lovely National Trust woods. It was run in a very authoritative way by a retired army colonel. We all got an enormous amount of exercise, but the bags were quite small, with generally a brace of pheasants or the odd partridge or duck to take home at the end of the day. But the shooting was not expensive and good fun.

Moving to the cottage in Wildmoor in 1979 brought me closer to a number of Hampshire shoots, and in the early 80s I was invited to join a local shoot run by Dwight Makins at Beau Repair. Dwight's father, Lord Sherfield, had been British Ambassador in Washington, and his mother, a charming lady, was American, hence the Christian name. It was a very nice little shoot with modest bags but limited topography. However it was a step up from Sussex and only ten minutes from the cottage.

That was the start of my more formal shooting, as before that I had relied on invitations from friends such as Rollo Denbigh at Newham Paddox and Jonathan Fenston, who had inherited the Druids Lodge Estate in Wiltshire from his father, Felix.

Jonathan was a most generous host. He entertained both his friends and his father's old friends regularly for two days' mid-week shooting of partridge and pheasant, putting everybody up in a large, slightly old-fashioned lodge. The lodge had formerly been owned and run as a racing stable by the J. Arthur Rank Organisation and was famous for glamorous parties with well-known starlets in the 20s and 30s. After the war the estate had been purchased by the Fisher family, who had leased it to Felix Fenston, who had an option to purchase the estate when the old lady died. That obviously helped to reduce death duties for the Fisher family.

The estate was subsequently sold by the Fenston Trust, but not before I had benefited from many two-day invitations to shoot, during which I met many of Felix's old shooting colleagues. There were such characters as Bobby Petre, who had ridden the winner of the Grand National as an amateur in 1954 on a horse called Lovely Cottage, the Clark Brothers chairman and the deputy chairman of Plessey, who were both shooting at Druids when GEC made a takeover bid for their company. I admired John's cool reaction; the news did not seem to affect his shooting at all. I had expected him to rush up to London. Another charming guest was Eric Bailey, whose three sons all subsequently became family friends and with whom I have enjoyed many years' fishing, shooting and skiing.

On a grouse moor, Castle Grant, 2006: Robert Cooper, self, Rollo McNally, Valentine Cecil, Pru Cooper, John de Ramsey, Alison de Ramsey, brother Paddy, Richard Cotterell, Fee Sangster, Nick Ryder, Charlie Egerton, Guy Sangster and sons, Ned, Milo

On moving to Upper Lambourne in 1987 I was invited to join the shoot at East Garston owned by Bill Tullock, the elder brother of an old friend, James, and a business partner of Charles Stuart Montleith, who had introduced me to Lloyds in the mid 70s. Bill Tullock had been an extremely successful entrepreneur, having made a fortune in the new issue market and on his Far East investments. This had enabled him to buy Gay Kidersley's farms in East Garston and the Glen Buchet Estate in Aberdeenshire, which included a substantial house and a 12,000 acre grouse moor.

Bill used to smoke like a chimney; sadly this led to his early demise from lung cancer. He and his wife Georgina were extremely good hosts, living just outside Highworth, and were never happier than when entertaining numerous family and friends. They also had been extremely successful with their horse racing, with horses Poldaro and Lan-e-ye (whose nickname was 'Lean on the Aga').

Bill has been succeeded by his son Freddie, who had to make the difficult decision as to which of the two estates to retain. Sadly Glen Buchet had to go, but luckily the estate at East Garston was kept and Freddie now runs the extremely successful Kimbers shoot there with Bruce Lindley, his excellent gamekeeper. The land has great topography, with partridge and pheasant presented to maximum effect. For over 20 years this has provided me with many days of superb shooting and great company.

Driving up to London after Georgina's funeral I was giving a lift to Jamie Riddell and Charlie Brooks when Charlie accidentally put petrol into my diesel car. We just made it to the Membury service station, where Charlie organised taxis and repairs to the car, generously paying for it all - a real trooper.

I have also been extremely fortunate in my brother Paddy's

success and his acquisition of an estate at Warneford near Highworth, where not only has the house been brilliantly renovated but the shoot has been improved dramatically in recent years despite the rather limited topography. I think I am extremely lucky to have such a successful and generous brother.

My first stag, from Brae Roy, near Spean Bridge, 2002

ON THE SLOPES

I have already mentioned my introduction to skiing in Austria in 1968 by my old friend Lawrence Lamport. It was the start of a major romance with the snow. Having started to ski at 35 I was never going to be an expert. Thanks to regular holidays since then I have become a reasonably proficient skier, although I am still not very confident off piste. Visiting the higher Austrian, French and Swiss resorts, I ended up going to Verbier in Switzerland, where since 1993 I have taken an apartment for a month each year, inviting members of the family and different friends to join me each week.

Taking a morning ferry from Dover, I usually drove out through France to arrive at the Swiss border in time for dinner in Malbuisson, just south of Pontallier at the splendid old Hotel du Lac, normally staying at the annexe Hotel Beau site. Close to the hotel there is a supermarket where after having breakfast we stocked up on wines and food for the apartment - it was a lot cheaper than Verbier - before the two-hour drive to the resort, where we collected the keys to the apartment Flamina on the Chemin de Verne. The apartment, built some 30 years earlier, has a wonderful view over the valley, with all four rooms opening out to the west-facing balcony. It has a principal combined reception, kitchen and dining room, three bedrooms, two bathrooms and a basement parking space as well as a parking area outside. The apartment was located some 200m below the main Médran lift, requiring a stiff walk up the slope each morning – one way to get the muscles going!

In 2011, having reached the age of 77, I became entitled to a free ski pass. It turned out to be a most expensive free pass. As I was escorting one of my guests down an easy pathway, my carving skis hit a block of ice and I found myself up in the air and crashing down on my hip. It transpired that the ball of the femur of my left leg had perforated the hip joint and smashed the pelvis. No wonder it was so painful!

After an operation in Sion, Switzerland, I was transported back to the UK, where the hip dislocated and a serious infection was diagnosed, requiring treatment for the rest of the year. This unfortunately led to the cancellation of shooting, fishing, tennis and most outdoor activities for over a year.

Skiing party, Verbier: Tim Gwyn Jones, Ginny Hoare, Angela Baring, PM, Angela Scott, a friend, Beatrice

On the slopes, 1995 - Liz Brewer, Judy Denbigh, Joanna and Louisa Barton

Skiing, Verbier 1998: Erica Porter, PM, Kristian Carmen, Lizzie Brewer, Peter Hunter

Verbier 2002, with Martin, Dick Barton, Louisa Barton, Joanna, Judy Denbigh and PM

EPILOGUE

I have been very fortunate in my life, in my family and my many friends. I have travelled extensively, seen much of the world and lived a very active and full life. Most important of all, I have enjoyed remarkably good health.

In retirement I have had the time and space to spend time on charitable projects and still enjoy fishing, shooting, skiing and partying.

With the help of my son Alexis I have created a charming garden in the house which I bought in Hannington Wick in 1997. The house had been built in the late 17th century, is listed Grade II starred, and had been modernised with great taste some twenty years earlier by the Wilson family. Since that time ownership had changed several times, probably due to the antiquated drainage system and the lack of a formal garden.

In 1995 I was lucky enough meet Beatrice, a talented gemmologist who makes lovely necklaces, at a drinks party given by my old friends Peter and Victoria Long. Some four years later she was to become my third wife - lucky for the third time! She had been married to a charming Frenchman, Remy Gimpel, from whom she had parted two years earlier. They have very talented twin sons, Erik and Marc. She lives in a charming old farmhouse in Drayton Gardens, built in 1790 and the oldest house in the road. Her parents, a very elegant couple, lived just outside Zürich in

Switzerland and had accumulated an amazing collection of modern and tribal art.

With Beatrice at a dinner

My third wife, Beatrice

We were married in Kensington and Chelsea Register Office in 1999, despite some delays due to previous bookings missing their time slots, making us arrive for our lunch at Boodles after all the guests. Beatrice has been a wonderful caring companion, especially after my skiing accident.

One of the very few areas in which we have disagreed is in relation to modern art and my belief that the work of a true artist should be difficult to replicate. I believe that the art establishment values innovation above technical excellence, with ludicrously high values being placed on the output of the likes of Damian Hirst and Tracy Emin – the blind leading the blind!

Art galleries are however an important element of our western culture and need to make a living. The world would be a duller place if they were to disappear like the emperor's new clothes!

The Manor at Hannington Wick, one of my more recent paintings

INDEX OF NAMES

INDEX OF NAMES

ND - #0187 - 270225 - C188 - 229/152/9 - PB - 9781909544550 - Matt Lamination